America From The Otherside Of The Tracks

Michael Feistel

Cover design by Sheila Passeiner
Edited by Ben & Marlene Kautz

WORK CITED

Yenne,Bill. The History of the Burlington Northern. New York: Bonanza, 1991. (52-93).

ISBN-10: 0615618383
ISBN-13: 9780615618388

ACKNOWLEDGMENTS

I'd like to give special thanks, Ben & Marlene Kautz for all their support and editing skills, most importantly for being friends. Ben and Marlene if wasn't for you pushing me so hard at the end, I might not have made it over the hump.

I'd also like to give a big thanks to Margret Hamill for her editing skills and computer knowledge. Margret thanks for being a friend.

I also want to thank Kristi Porter for all her help and support with Create Space. Thanks Kristi.

I'd also like to thank the White Lake writer's group for their support.

I'd also like to give special thanks to Lee Williamson, my former boss. Thanks for being there for me during a dark time in my life. Lee you're guidance helped turn my life around. Thanks again.

A special thanks to my family because you believed in me from the time I took on this venture. I love you all more than you can imagine.

HOBO CODE

As inscribed in the Annual Convention Congress of the Hobos of America held on August 8, 1894 at the Hotel Alden, 917 Market St., Chicago, Illinois;

1.-Decide your own life, don't let another person run or rule you.

2.-When in town, always respect the local law and officials, and try to be a gentleman at all times.

3.-Don't take advantage of someone who is in a vulnerable situation, locals or other hobos.

4.-Always try to find work, even if temporary, and always seek out jobs nobody wants. By doing so you not only help a business along, but insure employment should you return to that town again.

5.-When no employment is available, make your own work by using your added talents at crafts.

6.-Do not allow yourself to become a stupid drunk and set a bad example for local's treatment of other hobos.

7.-When jungling in town, respect handouts, do not wear them out, another hobo will be coming along who will need them as bad, if not worse than you.

8.-Always respect nature, do not leave garbage where you are jungling.

9.-If in a community jungle, always pitch in and help.

10.-Try to stay clean, and boil up wherever possible.

11.- When traveling, ride your train respectfully, take no personal chances, cause no problems with the operating crew or host railroad, act like an extra crew member.

12.-Do not cause problems in a train yard, another hobo will be coming along who will need passage thru that yard.

13.-Do not allow other hobos to molest children, expose to authorities all molesters, they are the worst garbage to infest any society.

14.-Help all runaway children, and try to induce them to return home.

15.-Help your fellow hobos whenever and wherever needed, you may need their help someday.

16.-If present at a hobo court and you have testimony, give it, whether for or against the accused, you voice counts!

A special note to the Reader:.

Now that you know the rules of the road, you need to get out that old backpack stored in your closet and blow the dust off it. Then throw in a couple of changes of clean clothes, a sturdy pair of hobo shoes, and expect to get some sand in them. Then pack a good warm bedroll, a warm coat, because it gets cold up in the mountains, and whatever else you think you might need for our journey. Now get ready to embark upon the adventure of a lifetime.

CHAPTER 1

"Of all times to screw up why. Now? I chastised myself. *My stupidity is going to cost me two days loss.* Another time it might not have mattered. But rumor had it, the cherry-picking season down in Lodi, California was about to come into play. Rumor had it, that if a person could pick fast enough, they'd be able to earn as much as a hundred bucks a day. If that was so, hobos were most likely flocking that direction. from all corners of the nation. I had somehow caught the wrong train out of Pasco, Washington and was now gazing down upon the Yakima valley carpeted with green rolling hills and, orchards in full blossom., with a shimmering river snaking across the basin floor. I could also make out snowcapped mountain peaks glinting against a cloudless back drop on the distant horizon.

If my plans would have gone accordingly, I would have already been in Wishram, my intended destination. With some luck, later that night, I would have caught out on the southbound California train, departing from the switchyard at around midnight, putting me in Lodi, in only a couple of days. Now hundreds of miles from Wishram, I knew I wasn't going anywhere. If memory served correctly, there wouldn't be another train departing out of the Yakima yard, going east, or west, until at least the next day.

Right about now you might be wondering how I came to riding freight-trains in the first place. And that is a reasonable question.

It all started as far back as my memory will take me. When I was a very young, my family and I lived in a house on Delphis Street, in Kokomo, Indiana. Every evening I'd lie snug in my bed, and anxiously wait to hear the freight-train rumble through town about the same time. As I lay there, I would not only wonder where the old freight was bound, but wished I was aboard, traveling to destinations unknown.

As I matured in years, I was reassured by my elders that this wander lust of mine would fade with time. However, as I aged, it became more intense. Even throughout my school years, I was constantly being scolded for gazing out the window, day dreaming of going to anywhere but where I was.

When I was twelve, my dad moved our family into a beautiful lake home in Whitehall, Michigan. Living on the lake was paradise for any young boy. Not only did woods surround the entire area behind our property, there was hunting, fishing, boating, among countless other activities available to entertain an adventurous young mind. The move made me hope that I'd keep active enough to put an end to the madness that unceasingly tormented me.

Arnie Mackie was the first kid I befriended in my new surroundings and before long we became best friends. Arnie and I had many grand adventures in his, 16' Thompson wood boat, equipped with a sixty five horsepower Mercury outboard motor. We ventured up the White River as far as that old boat would take us, until shallow water, stumps, and snapped shear-pins prevented us prevailing further. On warm summer nights we'd take his boat out into the big lake and camp out on the Lake Michigan beach. On moonlit nights we'd run wild through the giant sand dunes that closely guarded Lake Michigan's shoreline. We were always off on some crazy escapade, doing something we weren't supposed to. For the first time since I could remember, I was content, and even happy, to the point my wander lust problems began to subside. However, that all changed after Arnie introduced me to his father, Hugo Mackie.

Hugo was a full blooded Fin Lander. Like most Finns, Hugo had his own private sauna bath built on the White Lake shoreline. His sauna was equipped with a spacious three level steam room, a large outer lounge, with a dining table and chairs, bunk beds, a small refrigerator and a stove to boot.

Saturday night was always sauna night, an evening of relaxation and entertainment for Hugo and his cronies after putting in a long work week. Arnie and I were graced with the privilege of being take in a few heads of steam, he and his buddies able to hang out with Hugo's gang. After they'd would turn down the lights, kick back, drink a few cold ones, and share tales of their youth. Though I enjoyed listening to all of Hugo's friends' stories, his by far were my favorite. Hugo was an engineer for the Chessie System Railroad.

His tales always began with: "Back in 1948, when I was just eighteen, I was hired on with the Marquette Railroad as a fireman. "It was my job to shovel the coal into the belly of the old steam locomotive!"

Arnie would just look over at me, roll his eyes, and mumble, "Oh no! Not 1948 again."

But I never wearied of hearing his experiences, out on the steel rail, traveling between, Detroit, and Chicago. Every Saturday night, I'd sit on the edge on my seat, taking in his every word. In middle of one of his tales, he'd most always leap from his chair and prance around the room, stooped over, shaking his caboose. This was to demonstrate the technique and coordination it took to dance to the rhythm of the cross-tie waltz. I could always envision him shoveling the black coal into the blazing furnace, as the old steam locomotive screamed down the track at ninety plus miles an hour. As years past, I became more and more obsessed with the dream of traveling the nation by way of the silver rail.

The car lurched forward pulling me from my thoughts. The train was making the final descent down into the valley.

The sun beat down upon the tops of the railcars like an incinerator and the odor of creosote stifled the air. Since I was marooned, I thought I'd head over to the local Rescue Mission and try to cop -a-flop, and a couple of hots. I mopped my shirt sleeve across my sweat soaked forehead, and then I began weaving through the narrow corridors, in search of a way out of the labyrinth of surrounding steel cars.

Near the facility, I'd catch glimpses of men in shadowed alleys, passing bottles to each other. Outside the mission, transients were lined up for more than a city block. Some men leaned against the building, others sat along the curb, most with empty tombstone stares in their eyes, from drinking rotgut wine. It was a scene I was more than accustomed to. But the young kid, standing away from the crowd, however, caught my attention. I thought how out of place he looked in his present environment. He was wearing a cream-colored western-style shirt that had white pearl buttons down the front, and his Levi jeans and cowboy boots looked fairly new. Shorter than me, he stood around five four, with wide shoulders. His flip nose was sprinkled with freckles, and dark brown curly hair framing in his round face, set off by bright blue eyes. I couldn't get over how much he resembled a young version of Mac Davis.

When he realized he was being watched, he scowled at me. I took that as my cue to walk over and introduce myself.

"Mike's my name," I said.

"What's it to you?" he snarled. "You don't give a damn about me."

"I've been out here long enough to know you're not here because you want to be. In short, you stand out like a sore thumb amongst this crowd. But you seem to have everything under control, so I'll leave you alone," I said as I turned to walk away.

"Wait a minute Mister," he burst out, on the verge of tears. I need to find someone to help to get back to Dallas, Texas. That's where my dad lives"

"How do you propose I do that?" I said, turning to face him.

"You came in on the train, didn't ya?"

"Forget it kid. Riding trains is dangerous."

"I'm not afraid. Please give me a chance, I promise I won't give you no trouble," he pleaded. "You don't understand I have to get back to Dallas. I just have to."   "Try calling your dad? I bet he'd send bus fare if you just asked."

"He'd do it in a heartbeat," he said boastfully. "But there'd be trouble once he found out what happened out here. His heart ain't good you know. I can't take the chance of doing anything to upset him"

"You can't be more than fifteen."

"I am fifteen," he said bowing his head. "Why are you here anyway?" "I don't want to talk about it!" he snapped. I just have to get back to Dallas! "I can't go back there."

"Back where?" I asked, confused.

Tears streamed down his face. So I directed him away from the passing crowd.

He sobbed before regaining his composure: "My mom and I were doing ok until she met that no-good-son-of-a-bitchin' Earl. The bastard got her strung out on drugs and booze. Anymore, ma doesn't know her own name most of the time."

He swiped his shirt sleeve across his eyes.

"A couple of days ago the bastard made the mistake of hitting on her in front of me. That's when him and me went to fist city."

Apparently this Earl character roughed the kid up pretty bad. Then he tossed him out of his own mother's home, out onto the street, as though he were yesterday's garbage.

How could anybody get away with doing something like that to a kid? Then I remembered a friend, I had gone to junior high with had also been beat up by his mother's abusive alcoholic boyfriend. And nothing was ever done about it either. I wanted to go track down this S.O.B and knock the crap clean out of him. But I knew that would result in free lodging at the cross bar motel. It was clear the kid needed to escape his present plight. It wouldn't be long before pimps, among other predators would try to get their filthy meat hooks dug into him, if they hadn't already.

"Tell ya what; meet me out here in the morning. We'll figure something out. Cheer up, better days are ahead. Never did give me your name kid."

"Curtis," he said, making eye contact, breaking a smile.

Just then the mission door opened. We got in line and were ushered into the building for the mandatory ear banging.

The chapel was a large dank room, reeking of mildew. The walls were plastered with posters, with scripture verses printed on them. In the front of the chapel was an elevated stage, with a pulpit in the center. All the pews were jammed. The rest of the crowd stood along the walls. Curtis and I were wedged into a pew like sardines in the center of the commotion. As stinky men pressed in on both sides, my mind drifted to other thoughts. I was already regretting that I told the kid I'd help him get back to Dallas. To take a fifteen year old boy on a journey of that distance would be an incredible obligation. If riding rails had taught me anything, it was how quickly dangerous situations could pop up. Besides, I was down to less than fifty bucks in my pocket. I needed the cherry picking job. On top of everything else, if his mom were to start looking for him, I could get into a lot of trouble with the law. On the other hand, if I were to leave him, God only knew how his fate would end up. Yet, more and more, the thought of ditching the kid after breakfast crept into my mind. *He'll be okay,* I kept assuring myself.

My reverie was suddenly broken by an explosion.

"Who shit themselves?" someone shouted out.

In unison we all burst into hysterical laughter. But when the putrid stench blanketed over us, we were all gasping, and covering our noses.

The tall elderly gentleman, standing behind the podium didn't seem to find the situation too humorous, however. He scowled down at us pathetic sinners in disgust.

His white hair was slicked back and his bloodshot eyes were sunk behind white bushy eyebrows. Perched at the end of his long beak nose was a pair of reading spectacles. His attire consisted of a black undertaker's suit.

"Are we ready to hear God's word brothers?" his voice boomed through out the chapel. He then opened the service with the song *"The Old Rugged Cross,"* which most of us sang from memory? Afterward, the preacher-man engaged into a fire-and-brimstone sermon, reciting Bible verses that spoke of helping our brothers and looking out for one-another. "The Lord is close to the broken hearted; and those who are crushed in spirit he saves! Psalms 34:18." As the preacher's sermon unfolded, I began to feel heavily convicted for even considering the thought of abandoning the kid in his plight. One of the golden rules of the road was: "always help the homeless kid in need." When the preacher man quoted this next scripture verse, I swear he fixed his piercing gaze dead upon me: "If we wrong a refugee, widow, or orphan, and they cry out to God, He will surely hear their cry! Then God's wrath will flare to kill us with the sword! Exodus 22:22 -23."

A chill shot down my spine. I knew then and there, the spirit of the Almighty was speaking through this man, telling me to take this kid back to his dad's, in Dallas, or else. He then closed the service with the song, "The Old Rugged Cross."

Afterwards, we were ushered into a large room with tables and chairs. We were fed hot beef stew, bread, butter, and all the Kool-Aid we could drink. Curtis sat next to me. He wasn't about to let me out of his sight. Through the entire meal, I couldn't help to notice that an elderly man, one of the mission employees, gawked at me, in a way that made me feel very uneasy.

The same man, who had been watching me through the entire meal, pulled me aside as Curtis and I climbed the staircase leading up to the sleeping-quarters. He demanded to know what my intentions were with Curtis. According to him, the kid had been lodged at the facility for the last three days. He claimed he'd been keeping an eye on him whenever he couldm and his only concern was for the kid's welfare. I was leery to indulge my intentions to this man, yet my gut told his concerns were legitimate. So I revealed what I had in mind.

"Name is Tom," he said, as he shook my hand.

Tom was a big hulk of a man and when we shook, my hand felt small in his. His voice was deep like Johnny Cash's.

`"If you're taking the boy by rail, he's gonna need some travelin' gear. He only has a suitcase and no bedroll. After breakfast you boys meet me downstairs. I'll be waiting for you at the clothes closet the mission has for people in need. I'll do what I can for him. I'm an old tramp myself. Got off the road a spell to try and straighten my life out. I've only been here a couple of weeks, but I'm ready to blow this pop stand. They can take all their rules and stick em where the sun don't shine for all I care. Well, ya best git' up those stairs and take a shower."

A pale grey light streamed in through a window, from the streetlight outside, illuminating the lumps of snoring men snug in their cots. Curtis and I were among the fortunate to even get one to sleep on. Dozens of other's were forced to sleep on mats on the floor. As I lay there, the preacher's words resounded over and over through my head. How was I supposed to take a fifteen year old kid over two thousand miles through treachery and danger without getting busted or worse. Hitchhiking was out of the question. We wouldn't get far in the state of Washington before a cop ran a check on us. Then our trip would come to an end. More and more the thought of traveling by way of the rail, seemed to make the most sense. As dangerous as the rail could be, it seemed the only logical explanation. On the rail, we'd at least be able to keep a low profile, and stay clear of facilities requiring I.D. But crossing some of the higher mountain ranges without proper gear, that early in the season, could be lethal. This left me with no other choice but to take the long route to Texas. We'd have to travel down through Washington, Oregon, and then out across the desert, through California, Arizona, New Mexico, and finally Texas. A journey that distance would be a risky venture, to say the least.

Eventually the chorus of out-of-key snorers and the toxic gas explosions erupting all around me pulled me down into dreams of the adventures awaiting Curtis and me, around the bend.

Chapter 2

"Hit the showers, you lazy tramps!" I sprung up on my rickety cot and gawked around the room, not sure of my whereabouts. The configuration of sour faces, the stench of rancid feet, and raunchy farts quickly reminded me, I was in the mission.

Tom winked at me just before disappearing down the staircase.

fter breakfast Tom was waiting for us in front of the clothes closet. When he saw us coming, he immediately opened it. In just a couple of minutes he managed to scrounge up a pair of fairly new "Colorado" brand hiking boots that were almost a perfect fit for the kid. He also dug up an old blue backpack, a green winter coat, with white fir around the hood, and a White Stag sleeping-bag, still in fair condition, as well as two changes of clothes.

Although Curtis was more than thrilled with his new attire, he was determined to still wear his cowboy boots because his daddy had given them to him as a gift.

"Now listen here, you little peckerwood," Tom snapped, pointing his finger in his face. "You best change that cocky attitude before I box your ears. Put the damn boots in your pack and be done with it."

"Ok, Ok, I'll put em'em in my pack," he smirked.

"That's more like it. You do what Mike tells you, it might save your life. Riding trains ain't fun and games. You should be so lucky he's even taking you under his wing."

"Yes sir," Curtis said bowing his head.

We thanked Tom repeatedly for the kindness he had shown us.

"You boys, be careful out there, you hear? And take care of the kid," he said.

"I promise, I'll guard him with my life."

"That's what I wanted to hear."

"Maybe our paths will cross again someday," I said choked up. Then we turned, taking our first steps toward Curtis's homeward journey.

"I'll be looking forward to it," his voice trailed behind us.

On our way to the switchyard, Curtis skipped and ran ahead. We made a stop at a neighborhood grocery. There I picked up some beef jerky, a loaf of bread, and some treats. Out on the curb, wWe consumed the Twinkies, and chocolate milk. out on the curb. Afterwards, we divvied the goods between the two packs.

It didn't take long to find a hobo jungle hidden in a grove of trees near the tracks. Curtis searched for firewood, while I regrouped the stones back around the fire pit that former occupants had apparently strewn about the camp. Minutes later he returned, both arms full of dead branches. A few minutes later we had a fire going, and coffee pot on the grid.

Curtis had somehow managed to slip away while I busied with the fire. I spotted him swinging on a nearby railcar like it was a jungle Jim. I motioned for him. He strode back over, with a cocky grin, and then he plopped down on his pack. I winced, thinking there goes the bread.

"Yeah," he said with smugness in his voice. "What's up?"

"The last thing we need is to draw attention to ourselves. You
've got to sit and be still. I've got books. Try reading, it's a good pass time."

"Here, these are Louis L'Amour," I said, pulling a couple of tattered books from my pack. "They're easy reading. At least try before I'm forced to hurt you."

"Whatever!" Then he snatched the books from my hands and gawked at the pictures of cowboys and horses on the ragged covers.

We settled against our packs, sipped coffee and read. Shafts of the morning sun filtered down through the leaves, dappling the ground with green blotches, and birds chirped in the branches above us. It was a beautiful spring day.

Every so often, I'd glance over to see if Curtis was actually reading, or still looking at the pictures. Surprisingly, he appeared to be engrossed into his book.

The hypnotizing lull of a nearby lawnmower and the smell of fresh cut grass made me feel drowsy. I struggled to keep my eyes open, suspecting the kid would get into mischief the moment I dozed off, but my head kept bobbing. Then I'd jerk awake. Despite my efforts, my eyelids grew heavier and heavier.

"Mike! Wake up! Wake up! I hear engines out in the switchyard!"

"I must have dozed off," I said, rubbing my eyes. "How long have I been out," I asked groggily.

"A couple of hours."

Sure enough, I heard the rumble of locomotives out in the yard.

"Grab your gear, we're goin' to Seattle!" I exclaimed, as I snuffed the fire, and dumped out the remainder of the coffee. My heart raced with excitement while getting ready. As many trains as I had caught, it was always a thrill to me.

"Let's make for those railcars," I said. "Once inside them, we'll work our way toward the train."

"Let's do it," Curtis said, excitedly.

After climbing over several strings of cars, I motioned for Curtis to stop.

"See that man the next row over," I whispered. "He's working on our train. Let's wait here until he works his way further down the line. Most of these railroad workers are pretty cool, but let's not take any chances."

"That's our train?" Curtis said in awe.

"That's our baby!"

We squatted down and waited until the brakeman was well out of sight. Then we climbed over and walked to our train. Two idling locomotives were already hooked just a couple cars up from where we stood. We crept with stealth as we neared the green and white, Burlington Northern engines. When we reached the lead engine, we looked up toward the cab. As far as we could see, the crew wasn't intact yet. So I instructed Curtis to hurry up and walk around the lead engine and start walking toward rear of the train.

"Wow! These engines are huge when standing next to them," he exclaimed in awe.

"Actually, these are small compared to some of the bigger twelve wheeler road hogs."

"Wow all that power!"

As Curtis tiptoed in front of the lead unit, the air dryer kicked in and made a loud pssst. He literally almost jumped out of his skin.

"You did that on purpose," he sneered.

"You'll get used to it. Come on get moving before the crew shows up."

About twenty cars or so, down the line, Curtis shouted across, that there was an open car on his side.

"Let's keep looking. And keep your voice down."

A few more cars down we found ourselves gawking at each other through opposing doors. I thought how the old car looked beat up as I evaluated its interior.

"This is our ride kid!"

"There is an open boxcar on the other track, back a ways," he said, "with a bunch of cardboard inside it. This floor looks funky. I'm gonna run

24

back and grab a couple sheets to lay our gear down on."

"Alright, I'll keep an eye on the gear," I was impressed he even thought of it.

"You got it!" Then he tossed his pack up unto the deck and scurried away.

I grabbed hold of the door latch and swung up inside. I walked over to the other door and pushed his pack further away from the edge with my foot. That's when I noticed that the car leaned toward that side. Curious, I craned my head out the door. The logo, "*Great Northern,*" and the mascot, a majestic picture of a Rocky Mountain goat perched on top of a mountain crag, was faded and chipping. The sky blue paint on the side of the car was also stonewashed and peeling. A wooden plaque was on the side of the door. The thick piece of cardboard stapled to it, read, "OUT OF SERVICE." Inside the car, shafts of sunlight beamed down onto the old wood floor, through rips in the cars exterior skin. The walls were also bulged out, meaning the old car had most likely been in a derailment or two, during its long service with the Great Northern Railway. I wondered if the old relic might have even been around during the Depression. *If only these walls could talk,* I thought. What would they tell me? Would they share the countless awesome sunsets and sunrises it had witnessed through many years of rambling up and down the old cross-tie road? How I also longed to hear the many tales shared within the depths its carriage, by old hobos long gone, but not forgotten.

Only this nostalgic relic withheld the answers to my endless questions.

The sound of shuffling gravel snapped me from my reverie. Curtis was running toward the car with both arms full of cardboard.

"Good job." I said. Then I reached down and gave him a lift up.

"You should see all the stuff back there!" he huffed.

"This will do just fine. Let's move everything to the front for now. Once clear of the yard, we'll spread out near the door. Shhh, I thought I heard foot steps walking in the gravel."

"I thought I heard something too," Curtis whispered.

Suddenly a middle aged man poked his head inside the door, on the other side of the car.

"How's it goin' fellas?" he asked, as his eyes surveyed the interior of the car. "Are you sure you boys wanna' ride this decrepit old thing? I'm pretty sure it's on its way to the bone yard to be scrapped out. There are newer, cleaner open cars further down, toward the back of the train.

"We'll stick with this one," I said.

"Suit yourselves. Where are you boys off to anyway?"

I was about to give an elusive answer, when Curtis jumped up and blurted out, "We're going all the way to Dallas, Texas, Mister."

"It won't be long now before you're underway," he chuckled. "Be careful, and stay out of sight?" Then he ambled off.

The thought of danger reminded me of the doors. "We need a couple of railroad spikes, I only need two! Be quick about it!

Quite a few minutes later Curtis showed back up with both hands heaped with rusty old spikes.

"What took you so long?" I scorned him. "Hurry up and throw those down on the floor and give me your hand. This train is about to get underway anytime. After I gave him a lift up, I grabbed a spike and shoved it into a slot on the door track.

"These," I explained, "will hopefully help keep the doors from slamming shut if the train makes an emergency stop;" ...or is in an accident." Then I crossed the car. "Grab another spike and come over here and do the same thing I just did."

After he had jammed the spike into the right place, I said, "Good job. Now we're ready to rock-and-roll."

A couple minutes, we heard two toots of the horn, followed by a chain reaction of banging cars coming our way. Then our car jerked forward.

"We're fix'n to cannon-ball," I yelped.

Curtis ran over to the other door, poked his head and spouted the logos on the sides of passing railcars, "Great Northern! Burlington Northern! Northern Pacific! Spokane Portland and Seattle! Colorado and Southern! Burlington Route! Frisco! Fort Worth and Denver! Southern Pacific! Missouri Pacific! Northern Pacific! Rio Grande & Western!

Western Pacific! Union Pacific! Rock Island! Illinois Central Gulf! Chesapeake & Ohio! "

The car tossed and squeaked violently as it crossed over the multitude of tracks that joined together at the end of the yard. But once on the mainline, the car smoothed right out and glided along as smooth as a Cadillac.

I stood back inside the door and listened to the ding, ding, ding of the clanging railroad crossings zing past, and then fade away. Curtis ran from door to door waving gleefully at the onlookers sitting in their vehicles at the crossings.

We're jail bound for sure, I thought.

When the engines rounded a bend, I saw black clouds of smoke billow from the stacks, as the engineer opened the throttle. Soon the awesome power of those mega horse power diesels roared out across the open land and echoed off the nearby buildings, as the steel wheels beneath began to sing my favorite tune: Clickety Clack! Clickety Clack! Clickety Clack!

"Yee Haw!" I yelped. "We're railroading now baby!"

"I'm goin home! I'm goin home!" Curtis shouted repeatedly.

There couldn't be a more perfect day to embark upon an adventure, I thought as I gazed out toward the Cascades shadowing over the plain like silent guardians.

Chapter Three

Curtis and I were sitting crossed legged between the two open doors while we pored over my Rand McNally Railroad Atlas, discussing the various routes that could to take us to Dallas.

The Rand McNally Railroad Atlas was one of my prized possessions. Unlike the road atlas, it displayed the routes of railroads across the nation, rather than the highways and interstates.

Curtis continually pointed to the more direct routes that would take us over some of the higher mountain ranges. When I tried gently tried to explain to him that it was still too early in the season, because it got so cold up on top of some the passes at night, he copped an attitude.

"Which way should we go?" he sneered.

"Our safest bet, for this time of year would be to travel south, down the coast to Los Angeles, then out across the desert. Even though it's a great deal further, it's also much warmer taking that route. Besides, I wanted to take you to Wishram."

"What's so special about Wishram?" he snapped, as he snatched the atlas out of my hands.

"Wishram is a quaint railroad village nestled against the north bank of the Columbia River. Out of that yard is where many California trains are made up. Wishram is a major division point for the Burlington Northern. I don't think the village would even exist if it weren't for the railroad. The entire downtown consist of a, grocery store, bar and Laundromat all in the same building. Next to the tracks there's also a small café where railroad workers and hobos hang out, drink coffee and shoot the shit."

"So what, it sounds boring," he muttered, while trying to locate Wishram on the map's grid.

"Maybe to you it doesn't sound like much. I guess Wishram is more of a peaceful place where hobos are always made to feel welcome there.

"You got anything better than that?"

"On a clear day Mount Hood looms on the horizon like a picture postcard. Strung along the bank of the old Columbia are dozens of hobo jungles. The main reason Wishram is so highly favored among hobos, is because the Burlington

Northern track runs along the north bank, and the Union Pacific, runs along the south bank of the Columbia. Between the two roads, every night you are lulled to sleep by the sweet symphony of the clickety clack of the steel wheels, and the constant wailing of the lonesome whistle echoing down the box canyon for miles. Wishram also has some of the best star gazing I've ever found in all my travels. I'm here to tell ya, there's no other place like it on God's green earth."

"Maybe we should check this place out." Curtis said, trying to act all cool, as though he wasn't the least bit interested.

Evidently, something I said must have grabbed his attention though. "Who knows maybe we'll even hang out there for a couple of days and do some Cat fishing in the old Columbia?"

"Let's go to Wishram!" he shouted.

Then I snatched the Atlas back and put it away. While in my pack, I pulled out a bowl, a spoon, and a tin cup, and handed them to him.

"Here, take these, they are vital for survival out on the road. Especially, when invited into a jungle. Most hobos assume that you have your own bowl and spoon.

"Thanks," he said, then he stowed them away. "I'm done with the books already. Got anymore?"

"As a matter of fact I do." I pulled a couple more Louis L'Amour from my pack and handed them to him.

"I guess I'm gonna go read. There ain't nothin' else to do." Then he stretched out, near the door, on his bedroll with his head propped against his pack and opened another book.

It had been a while since I'd made an entry into my journal. So I pulled it from my pack and read my last admission.

At that time I had been up in Orville, Washington pruning fruit trees in the orchards. Orville was only a couple miles south of the Canadian border. There was where I heard about the cherry harvest soon to come into play down in Lodi, California. Since the pay wasn't all that great where I was, I decided to head south. That evening I got what money I had coming to me. The next morning, I caught the local southbound train out of Orville, down into Wenatchee. From there, I caught a mainliner over to Pasco. Pasco was where I grabbed the wrong train and ended up in Yakima.

Yesterday my life took a bizarre turn, as it often does out here on the open road. While on route to Lodi, California, I caught out on the wrong train out of Pasco, Washington, and ended up in Yakima, hundreds of miles from Wishram. My path happened to cross with a kid whose name is Curtis while I was lodged at the local rescue mission. Although Curtis desperately needed help to get back to Texas, I had my own issues to deal with and didn't want to take on the burden. However, after hearing the wild sermon delivered by the preacher man that evening, I was led to believe, I was being called, by God himself, to take this kid under my wing and return him home safely to his dad in Dallas, Texas.

With the help of the kindly older gentleman named Tom, who was temporarily employed at the mission, we were able to begin Curtis's homeward quest with the proper road gear for such a long and perilous voyage. Tom is a big husky man., who at first came across with a gruff ornery disposition, but turned out to have a heart of gold. He very much reminds me of my grandfather, on my mother's side.

Amazingly, Curtis seems somewhat happy-go-lucky in spite the rotten hand of cards life has dealt him. God willing, I'll get him home safely. Hopefully, returning him to his father will bring a positive change in his messed up life. I can only hope. Maybe I'll never know. Maybe I'm not meant to.

I set down the journal, stood up and stretched. Curtis was asleep with a book covering his face. I walked over to the door and poked my head out to let the free wind blow through my hair. I was awed at how the Cascade's had grown so much larger as the miles melted away. As many times as I witnessed their grandeur, I was always mesmerized by their majesty. Eventually I pulled myself away and then stretched out on my bedroll and read until swept away by the steady drone of the rumbling wheels beneath: Clickety Clack! Clickety Clack! Clickety Clack!

Chapter 4

The loud pssst, from the engines breaking away from the train snapped me awake. I didn't think much about it. But when the car began to roll backwards the hairs bristled on the back of my neck. Backwards almost always meant being switched off on a side track. I sprung up.

"Move it kid!

"What's wrong?" he said, rubbing his eyes.

"I think we are being switched off! Now move your ass!"

I jumped up, and ran over to the door in frenzy.

"That's far enough," said a man's voice. I assumed that he was speaking to me, until I realized he was talking into a walkie talkie. Then the car came to a squeaky stop.

"What's goin' on?" I gasped, gawking up and down the track like a madman.

"We're busting her in half," said the young brakemen. "We're dragging more tonnage than these two old girls can pull over the hump. In short, the railroad's too cheap to give us enough power to get the job done."

"Where are we," I asked, still half out of it.

"Cle Elam," he said, trying to slip his walkie talkie back into its clip.

"You mean you're coming back?"

"That's right. We'll pull the other half of the train over the hump, drop it off in a siding, and then double back. You'd be smart to stay down here. It gets damn cold up on top of the pass after dark this time of year. Where are you guys off to?" he asked.

"We're goin' all the way to Dallas, Texas," Curtis blurted out as he came up behind me.

A faraway look flickered in the man's eyes. "Sounds like an adventure. If I didn't have a family, I just might be inclined to grab my backpack and tag along."

Static broke over the walkie talkie, "Are you ready?" said a crackly voice.

"I'm ready," answered the brakeman. "Duty calls boys. See ya in a bit." Then he scurried off, still trying to secure the walkie talkie into the belt clip.

Since we weren't going anywhere for a while, I thought that that would be a good time to try and do some laundry, if there was a facility in the vicinity.

"What ya say we try and find a Laundromat close by to wash your sleeping bag and coat since we don't know where either of them have been. Then we'll grab a couple of burgers, and fries before our train gets back."

"I'm starved," he said rubbing his belly.

"Why doesn't that surprise me.?"

We managed to find a laundry only a couple of blocks from the yard that was even equipped with a super sized washer. Along with the sleeping bag and coat we tossed in everything else that was soiled into the super sized washer. Curtis picked up a Field and Stream magazine and plopped down on a chair, while I finished stuffing the rest of the clothes into the machine. Then I placed the coins into the slots, shoved them in. Once the machine was started we took off to find someplace to grab a bite to eat.

We found a bar a couple doors down from the laundry that had tables and chairs to sit down at. When we walked in there was a tall, thin, sickly looking middle-aged man stooped over a sink washing glasses. Besides him, we were the only other people there.

"What's your poison boys?" he asked.

"Two cheeseburgers, two fries and a couple of Cokes," I replied.

He wiped his hands on a towel, and grabbed a couple of longneck Cokes from the cooler, popped the tops, and then delivered them to our table.

"Those burgers will be up in a few, gents," he said over his shoulder, as he headed for the grill.

The meat searing on the grill set my stomach to growling and my mouth to watering. A few minutes later the old barkeep brought over two plates of steaming burgers, with cheese melting down the sides. We snatched the burgers from the plates, practically before they even hit the table and commenced to gobbling them down. The bar tender then brought over two separate plates heaped with steaming golden brown french-fries. After I literally devoured the burgers, we started in on the fries. Then we washed them down with the ice cold cokes. We were just finishing up the last of our fries when the barkeep brought another round of Cokes to the table.

"These are on the house, boys," he said with a sad smile. Then he pulled up a chair and sat down.

"I've got a son about your age," he said, looking Curtis over. "Don't see him much though. His ma left me a few years back. Couldn't take no more of my drinkin'. Now I'm an old tramp myself," he said, as he look over toward our backpacks propped up near the door. "I move around a lot. Never stay no place too long. Lost my license a few years back. Now when I get the notion to move, I grab my old suitcase and look for the Grey Dog."

"What's the grey dog?" asked Curtis.

"Greyhound!" the old timer laughed.

"I knew that."

"Where ya boys headed?"

"We're goin all the way to Dallas Texas," Curtis said boastfully.

"I'd say you have quite a journey a head of you then. Take some advice from an old fool. Stay the away from the booze, or it will eventually take everything that is good away from you in life." For a moment I thought he was going to tear up. Then he stood up and walked back over behind the bar and went about washing glasses.

"What's your name, sir?" I asked.

"James."

"James, I propose a toast that your son comes to visit you very soon."

"I second that," Curtis chimed in. Then Curtis and I knocked our bottles together, and James picked up a glass of soda.

"Here's another gift," he laughed, slapping the check down on the bar.

I paid the bill. Then we said farewells to our new found friend and thanked him for the free cokes and his comradery.

"Be careful out there boys," he called out as the door slammed behind us.

Alpine and fresh cut lumber scented the chill evening air and plumes of steam rose from our warm breath as we walked in silence back toward our boxcar. A lone coyote sang to the coming night in the distance and the tires of eighteen wheelers moaned a sad refrain from nearby interstate. The sun had already slipped behind the mountains, silhouetting them in a brilliant amber backdrop, and the planet Venus shone brightly in the twilight sky. A chill shot through me when the lonesome whistle suddenly pierced the evening solitude.

"I think that's our train?" Curtis shouted with glee.

"That's our sweet chariot calling our names."

We had no more got back to the boxcar when we watched two locomotives and the caboose barrel around the bend. Our car was directly in front of the caboose after the train was hooked up.

When we blew out of Cle Elum like a shot, our boxcar groaned and squeaked and slammed into the curves like a thrill ride at a theme park. I knew the engineer was getting a running start before hitting the grade.

Curtis clutched the side of open door with his head hung out, repeatedly yelping, "I'm going home."

"Get away from that damn door, you moron," I screamed over the racket. I was terrified the idiot would be ejected out the door like a rag doll at any moment.

Not long after the engines bent into the grade, our thrill ride soon slowed down to a snails crawl. Shortly following, a colossal bright orange half moon rose over the mountain tops, illuminating the landscape around us to almost as bright as day. Curtis and I watched intently from the boxcar door as the tracks skirted the edge of a moonlit valley carpeted with Ponderosa Pines, drooping with freshly driven snow. A shallow river snaked across the basin floor that shimmered under the moonlight like molten gold.

Shortly after clearing the hump, the train slowed down even more.

"Look," Curtis said pointing. "I think that's the other half of our train sitting on a side track."

Once the car cleared the other track, our car backed into the lead car on the other track. We hit with a jolt when the two halves reconnected back to each other. Once hooked up again, our car was near where the two tracks joined together.

"Where's the caboose?" Curtis said in bewilderment.

"That's a good question, where is the caboose?"

Just then we heard a loud clicking echoing down the moonlit canyon. Curtis stopped tying his shoes and I dropped the stick of gum I was about to pop into my mouth, when we both looked up the canyon saw the caboose speeding down the other track like a bat out of hell, straight toward our boxcar. Two trainmen were standing on the platform outside. One of them was cranking the round handbrake on the back of the caboose, while the other stooped over the railing, swinging a railroad lantern back and forth in a slow motion. As the runaway caboose streaked straight toward our car, the lantern illuminated his eerie ghostly face. Not more than fifty feet from our car the caboose finally came to a loud squeaky halt. Both men laughed hysterically when they saw the terrified looks on our faces.

"You guys are out of control," Curtis yelped.

Then our car jerked forward. Curtis and I waved and shouted yeehaws up the canyon as our car pulled from the caboose. A few minutes later, we felt a thump, when the caboose reattached to the rear of the train.

After all the excitement was over a bone depth chill hit me.

"I think we should pull our gear to the front of the car and try to get some shuteye."

"Do we have to?" Curtis protested.

"We're gonna need some sleep. We don't know what to expect on the other side. For tonight, I'd like for you to crawl inside my bedroll. You'll freeze in that flimsy thing of yours."

My dad had given me the old army issue goose-down sleeping-bag, supposedly durable of temperatures down to forty below zero. Carrying the old bag seemed a burden at times, but it had never failed to keep me warm, even under most the extreme conditions. It had become so much a part of me, that I would have been devastated to ever part with it.

"Are you sure it's ok?" Curtis asked.

"Just do what I tell ya for once, ok."

He burrowed down inside the old sack, content as a bug in a rug, wearing an ear to ear grin.

"You should be so lucky. You're the only person I've ever let sleep in that bag. So don't get too cozy. Now let's get some sleep."

When I crawled into Curtis's bedroll, I realized just how light it was compared to mine. I was thankful, though, for the cardboard Curtis had salvaged for us back in Yakima. It kept the bag off the icy floor.

I was almost asleep when Curtis asked, "How long do you think it will take us to get to Dallas?"

"That depends."

"Depends on what?"

"Many things. Riding freights isn't like taking Amtrak. If I were to take a guess, maybe a couple of weeks give or take."

"Do you think we'll get there okay?"

"How the hell do I know? Now get some sleep!"

I wondered about James back at Cle Elum as I lay there. His life seemed so sad and hopeless. I could envision him living in a small grungy apartment above the bar. Most likely, he drank himself into a stupor every night until he passed out, only to repeat the sad dilemma every night to follow. What disturbed most, was that all his dreams and hopes seemed to be shattered, leaving him with nothing but a hollow shell. *What is there to look forward too, if we don't have our dreams*?

As the train descended off the mountain side, the high pitched screeching of brakes was so unbearable, it was tough to fall asleep. But the good note was the air steadily grew warmer as we dropped altitude.

Chapter 5

Lights shinning into the car jerked me
awake. I yawned, stretched, then jumped up and
stumbled toward the door. As I poked my head out,
I was stood awestruck at how all the millions of
glittering winking lights carpeting the giant foothills
surrounding Puget Sound, reflected out onto the
glassy surface of the water front like a picture
postcard.

The train glided along on top of a levy, on
the outer edge of a sleepy Seattle suburb. As I
peered out over some of the fences of the backyards
bordering the base of the embankment, a pang of

loneliness overcame me. Swimming pools, bicycles, basketball hoops, among other kids toys, reminded me some colleagues I had gone to high school with, had already graduated from college, and started families of their own.

The car rocked, jerking me from my reverie. I looked around. The engines had already cleared the traffic signal at the throat of the switchyard, and were bound for the arrival yard that was at least a mile and a half back down the track from the only hobo jungle I had knowledge of in that area. Most all trains stopped for clearance before entering the yard, apparently not this one. The plan was to bale off when the train stopped for the clearance light. From there we'd hoof it over to the hobo jungle located under a high overpass bridge that spanned the width of the switchyard. I knew once the train slipped into the thick steel maze of railcars that lay just ahead, it'd be nearly impossible to bail off on the fly without one of us getting hurt, or worse. Since I had no intention of walking any further than we had to, I barked orders for Curtis to get up, el pronto, and start packing.

He groaned a bit, and then sat up. "What's wrong?" He said, rubbing his eyes.

"We're gonna have to bail on the fly! Get a move on!"

Still half asleep, he started throwing his things together.

While making his way toward the door, Curtis staggered like a drunken sailor, as the car rolled over a multitude joining tracks at the throat of the yard.

"Now toss your pack out with the flat side down," I shouted over the screeching wheels. "That'll keep it from bouncing under the train. Never jump where the tracks join together, or you could get your foot caught between the track and the wheels. That wouldn't be pretty. Now sit down in the door and dangle your legs over the side. Then grab the door latch! Lastly, drop down and get your feet going as fast as they'll carry you, at the same time, push away from the car, and be quick about it!"

"That's not the way it's done in the movies," he protested.

"This ain't the movies, boy. Now move your ass!"

He shouted, "Geronimo!" as he dropped into the pocket. Once his feet were in motion, he pushed away from the car like a pro. I leaned out the door and gave him the thumbs up. Then I tossed my pack out, and sat down into position and watched the blurred ground zing past, waiting for the precise moment to make my move. Then I dropped. All was well until I snagged my foot on a large stone and almost tumbled head over heels.

Curtis ran over: "Are you ok?"

"I'm fine!" I said agitated. *I'm supposed to be the expert.*

"That was bitchin!" he exclaimed. "I can't wait to do it again."

"Nothing fazes you kid."

When I went to pick up my gear, I discovered that a stone had punched a hole in the water jug, and all our precious water was leaking out onto the ground. "It just keeps getting better and better," I grumbled.

Both trainmen were standing on the back platform of the caboose when it ambled on past us. The same man we had spoken to back in Cle Elum said, "Good luck." Then he tossed a paper bag out toward us. The other man just stood there with a wide grin. We thanked them for the show they put on for us, back on top of the mountain, just before they vanished into the maze of railcars. Then Curtis ran over and picked up the bag. To our delight, inside was a huge turkey and cheese on rye sandwich, accompanied with six small bottles of partially frozen water.

"I'm glad we jumped when we did," I said pointing. "The jungle is under the far end of that bridge just a couple hundred feet behind us. It's next to one of the cement abutments. But we need to be extra careful though; I heard a switch engine rumbling out there somewhere.

"I'm ready to go," Curtis said, as he slung his pack over his shoulder.

We crept beneath the shadow of the bridge, climbing strings of railcars. We were just about to cross an open track, when I straight armed Curtis, hitting in the chest. His eyes grew as big as saucers when a string of free wheeling railcars zinged past, inches from our noses, followed by an earsplitting crash.

"That is a prefect example of how treacherous these switchyards can be if you are not paying attention."

"Shew! That was close!"

"Too damn close!"

After the switch engine hooked onto another string of railcars and began tugging, its mega horsepower motor screamed out in agony. We waited for the cars to clear the track in front of us. Then we dashed across.

"Let that be a lesson to you! When ever you're in a railroad yard, always use extreme caution. Floaters are how people get dead. They're referred to as floaters, because they're near impossible to hear, when rolling from either direction. Whatever you do, never walk on a clear track in a yard or anywhere else for that matter. Always walk beside it. By the time a floater creeps up, it's too late."

"Look," Curtis said, "someone is burning a fire on the other side of the bridge."

Near the jungle, we peered out between two railcars. As far as we could see, there was only a single, elderly man, hovering over the fire. He was wearing a long, dark frock type coat that extended almost down his shins.

"Some of these old timers prefer to be left alone," I whispered. I was contemplating if we should even bother him until the rich aroma of soup floated past our noses.

"Maybe we should at least go talk to this guy," I said.

"Now that's what I'm talking about," Curtis said, smacking his lips and rubbing his belly.

Before entering the camp, I kicked a rusty bucket, on the side of the path, to alert the old timer someone was approaching. When suddenly I was knocked clean off my feet, onto my back, and was gaping down into a dark tunnel of narrowly fangs. Hot stinky breath pressed against my face like a blast furnace and saliva spewed from long snapping teeth only centimeters from my throat. I thought I was a dead man, until I heard the elderly gentleman reprimand the beast to back off. As the black monster backed slowly away, crouched, snarling and snapping its teeth, my heart felt as though it were going to explode!

"Son, you don't know how close ya just came to dyin,'" said the old timer, as he reached out and gave me a lift to my feet. "Old Bear has been with me for dern near eight years now. He's gettin' old. He didn't hear ya comin'. Why you startled him from his nap. He came at ya as mean as a Grizzly awoked' from hibernation. My name is Buzz, and this is Bear. But ya two have already been introduced right proper," he laughed, slapping his thigh. Bear was the biggest, meanest, blackest, Newfoundland dog I had ever seen. The beast actually looked like a small black bear.

"Names Mike," I said, extending my trembling hand.

The old timers grip was strong and true. He stepped out of the fire light, momentarily returning with two buckets for us to sit on.

"Hope ya got spoons, because old Buzz has got some of the meanest stew this side of the Missisip, simmerin' in the gunbolt as we speak."

Curtis and I quickly fished out our bowls and spoons.

"Where ya from son?" Buzz asked Curtis.

"Dallas Texas," he answered boastfully.

"I knew there was somethin' I liked about ya boy. I'm a Texas man myself. Born and bred. And damn proud of it."

"*Arrogance must be a Texas trait,* I thought. In all my travels I had never met a Texan who wasn't proud to be from the great state of Texas.

Curtis being from Texas seemed to delight the old timer.

Curtis and I watched him like two hunger crazed wolves when Buzz ladled out two steaming bowls of thick chunky stew.

"This is bodacious!" Curtis said with his mouth full.

"It's the best, I've ever had," I agreed.

Buzz sat on his bucket with his hands behind his head, grinning from ear to ear, while gloating in his glory.

On Curtis's third helping, he rubbed his belly. "If I eat another bite, I'll explode he groaned. Then he set his bowl on ground.

"Would it be ok to give Bear the rest?" he asked.

"Old Bear would love ya for it son," Buzz chuckled. "Why you'll have a friend fer' life."

The words were barley out of Curtis's mouth when the beast sprang to his feet as agile as a pup. It then inhaled the remaining stew with what seemed like a single swipe of his massive tongue. Then he lapped his food soiled jowls until they were licked clean. But that didn't disgust me as much as when he walked over to Curtis, stared at him eye to eye, and then gave him a big slobbery kiss across the face. Curtis laughed, while scratching the beast behind the ears. Bear barked playfully in want of more attention. But Buzz reprimanded him to lie back down. He obeyed immediately.

"See that building down yonder," said Buzz.

Bubba and I stood up and looked in the direction he was pointing. I could make out an old building hidden partially in the shadows.

"Yeah, I think so," I said.

"I can barely see an old building," said Curtis.

"That ther' is the old round house."

"What's a round house?" Curtis asked.

"The roundhouse was used to turn the old steam locomotives around to go the other direction. I've been ridin' up and down these old rails since the Great Depression, and I ain't growd' tired of 'em yet. The days of steam was down right romantic, differnt era altogetha.' It used ta' be a better life out here, but so much has changed in the last thirta' years. These is some different times fer sure. I don' know what to think about this new genaration' of train riders. Thirty years ago, a tramp could leave his gear in the jungle and come back a week lata' and it'd still be there.

Anymore, if ya turn around, it's a good chance it won' be there when ya turn back. The code of the road used to be, leave the jungle in betta' shape than what ya found it. But these youngsters now days don' seem ta' have no respect for nobody. They get all drunked up and walk around the yard and upset railroad folks, makin' it tough on the rest of us. Then they bust their booze bottles all over, not thinkin' they have to sleep in ther' own mess. And before they leave, they tear the place up. Mark my word, ridin' trains will be a thing of the past someday.

That's sad because railroads are the history of this here great nation. If it weren't fer' them, there wouldn't be no history at all. Why one of the greatest days this country ever knowd' was May 10th, 1869, the day the Union Pacific and Central Pacific joined together at Promontory, Utah. Promontory is where the golden spike was driven', to form the first transcontinental road that spanned this here great nation, from sea to sea. That was the beginning' of a new era, not ta mention, one of the greatest accomplishments ever knowd' to man, at least back in them days. Irishmen built the road from the east? They spanned gorges, rivers, even canyons and fought hostile Injuns' ta boot. While the Irish built west, the Chinese coulees built east, from Sacramento, California."

The switch engine continued to rumble out in the switchyard, followed by crashes, while Buzz continued to educate us on American railroad history.

"The Chinese had to blast through those damn old Sierras in some of the worst conditions. Some days they'd be lucka' to gain a few feet. It was slow goin' until they conquered them mountains. But eventuala' the road was completed. What had takin long treacherous months to cross this here great nation, then only took a few days. From that point on, droves of settlers moved west as thick as flies on a cow patty. Many good men died buildin' the first transcendental road across this here great nation of ours," he concluded with sadness.

"Tell us more!" Curtis said.

Buzz was tickled we had taken an interest in the history of American railroads.

"This here road yer on is part of a dream of, James J. Hill, why Mista' Hill went down in histra' know'd' as the "Empire Builder. He devoted near most of his life buildin' one of the greatest railroads ever know'd', "the Great Northern Railway." Mista Hill was a true visionary. He once stated that the greatest adventure in his life was building the Great Northern Railway. There's never been another man in histora' who influenced American railroads as much as, James Jerome Hill."

"I thought we are on the Burlington Northern," Curtis blurted out.

"That's right perceptive of ya son," said Buzz. It's tough to fool a Texan. It so happens, on March 2, 1970, the Great Northern merged with the Northern Pacific, Chicago Burlington & Quincy, and the Spokane Portland, & Seattle roads, to form what is now know'd' as the, "Burlington Northern Railway."

The rumbling switch engine and crashes were silent by the time Buzz had finished his presentation on American railroads.

"If yer' ridin' trains," Buzz said." It's only propa' ya both have hobo names. I was once elected Hobo King at the National hobo convention, back in Britt, Iowa," he said boastfully. I have the authorita' to Knight a brother hobo at their request. Curtis, if it's ok with ya, I'd like to give ya the name, Bubba Lee. I've always been fond of that name. I think it suits a Texas man just fine."

"It's ok with me," Curtis said excitedly.

"For ya Mike, I haven't come up with nothin just yet.

" Ya just can't give any old name. It has to fit the person you're givin' it to."

"My younger sister, Marcia, calls me Free Bird, because I've been known to disappear from time to time and go off and have adventures.." And tThe name has kind of stuck with me through the years."

"Free Bird it is, I think it suits ya just fine. Boys stand up and face me."

After Curtis and I stood up, Buzz tapped our shoulders with his long fire poking stick and said, "Bubba Lee and Free Bird I now pronounce ya Knights of the open road."

Curtis strutted around the campfire repeating his new road name over and over. Bear lifted his head, growled and showed his teeth. Bubba plopped back down on his bucket. Then the beast lay back down on his paws and pretended to sleep. I knew figured that night would be imprinted into the kid's memory for the rest of his days. Maybe even for the first time in his life, he might have felt as though he were someone of importance.

It had been a long day and it suddenly hit me like a sludge hammer. I yawned, and then rolled out my bedroll near the fire. Then I propped my head up against my pack. A couple minutes later Bubba began to yawn. Then he rolled out his bedroll.

"Buzz, would ya share some your railroad stories, about you and Bear riding the rails all across America," Bubba pleaded.

"Do ya really wana' hear my borin' old railroad tales son?"

"Please!" Bubba begged.

"Can't rightly say no to that."

Sparks drifted lazily up into the bridges charred rafters above when Buzz tossed more wood into the fire. The fire light enhanced the deep grooves etched into his face from the many years of living out on the road as he poked and prodded with his long stick. Then he stood up, paced, while rubbing his chin, in thought.

As Buzz's tales unfolded there was a touch of magic inmagic in the air. I was held spellbound by the enlarged shadow of his long over coat swooshing and swaying in harmonic motion against the cement abutment, as he moved around the ring of fire

with the grace and ploy of a ballerina.   Buzz was a
master story teller. When ever he'd mention Bear's
name, the old dog would lift his head and blink into the
fire, and stare at his master with loving eyes, as though
 he was reminiscing of the time and place of that
particular occurrence. Then he'd whimper and lie back
down pretending to sleep again.

 In the middle of Buzz's tale, the lonesome
    whistle   echoed out across the void.
 The old timer stood as still as a stone, with his
hand perched over his ear. He hearkened to the call
of the lonesome whistle, with a far away gaze was
in his eyes. I knew he was no longer with us. Buzz
was frozen back in time, in the days of steam. After
the last clickety clack was swallowed into the night
silence, Buzz leaned in toward the fire. He said :
"Clickety Clack, rickety rack, clang, clang, then he
proceeded on with his tale.

Chapter 6

The quaking ground beneath, shook me awake. I sprung up and gawked around the perimeter of the camp, looking for danger. The disturbance was only a southbound freight rumbling past out on the mainline. The morning chill enticed me to recoil back down inside the warmth of my old down sack, but we had a big day ahead of us. Reluctantly, I slipped out, hopped into my jeans, and tossed some more wood onto the glowing coals. I poked and prodded with Buzz's long stick until the flames slowly licked the sides of the boards. As I went to put on morning coffee, I noticed there was still stew left in the gun boat from the night before. I scotched it in next to the coffee pot, thinking that it was gonna be a great day.

After pouring my first steaming cup, I sat down on a bucket and watched first light slowly silhouette the old roundhouse and the long strings of rail cars out in the switchyard. By then vendoer trucks were already racing up and down nearby streets, delivering fresh breads and coffee to local merchants. Morning traffic had also begun to amble over the bridge above, as America rose from slumber. Suddenly it occurred to me there was no sign of Buzz or Bear. *They could* be *out taking an early morning stroll, or they might have even caught the midnight train to anywhere U.S.A...*

I nudged Bubba and told him to get up.

"Leave me alone," he groaned.

"Come on, we have a big day ahead of us."

"Can I sleep a bit longer?"

"Go ahead, but there's no guarantee there'll be any stew left when ya get up."

He sprung up like a jack-in the box. "Did you say stew?"

"Yeah and it's better than last night."

He sprang out from beneath his bedroll, danced on one foot, trying to slip into his jeans.

"Where's Buzz and Bear?" he asked, rubbing his eyes.

"I don' know. When I got up they were nowhere to be found."

"Oh," he said disappointed. "Maybe they'll come back."

"I hope so."

We polished off the remainder of the stew and downed a pot of coffee, but there was still no sign of Buzz or Bear. So we waited around a bit longer, before deciding it was time to get moving.

Buzz had forewarned us about a railroad detective who roamed that part of the yard from time to time. So we walked among the cover of the railcars. Surprisingly they were still cool from the night before. But that would change when the sun climbed high enough to smile down upon them.

A mile or so down the line, we came upon a place where the inside rails were all empty, but the outside rails were occupied with strings of cars on both sides. In the center of the tracks there was a lean-to that was about five feet high and six feet wide, barely wide enough for the old beat up car seat inside it. Sitting next to the structure were two, one gallon containers of partially frozen water. I scanned the area. But no one seemed to be around.

"It's break time," I said.

"I'm all for that."

I dropped my pack, then latched a hold of a jug and took a long pull, until I got a brain freeze.

"That hit the spot," I said, rubbing my throbbing head.

Bubba snatched it from me and took a long drink himself. Then we plopped down on the old car seat and shared the turkey on rye sandwich the brakeman had tossed out to us the night before.

"How much longer before we get to that departure yard?" Bubba said with his mouth full.

"Not too much longer."

"These stones are killing my feet."

"Be glad you're not wearing your cowboy boots, or misery would have a whole new meaning."

For once he didn't come back with a smart ass comment.

"Maybe it's time we move on. I'm beginning to get an uneasy feeling we're either being watched, or someone is nearby."

"Me too, but this jug is goin' with us," Bubba retorted.

I didn't like taking anything that didn't belong to us, but ours had been destroyed the night before, we needed it. I dug out a piece of rope, and tied the jug to Bubba's pack.

A little further down the line, I began to notice the air hoses on the cars, on both sides of us were all coupled together.

"We might already be in the departure yard," I said. "Look all of the air hoses on both sides are coupled together, indicating these trains are already made up."

"What's that hissing noise? "Bubba asked.

"That sounds like a train about to get underway. And it's close"

Just then a string of cars, a couple of rows over, lurched forward. We hopped over two rows of railcars to get to it. The tracks were so close together, it was going to be tough to maneuver within the narrow isle. I even had doubts we'd be able to catch out if the train were to pick much more speed, before we were able to find anything to ride. I was almost to the point of letting it go," until I spotted an empty flatcar rolling our way.

"Drop your pack," I yelled. "Then grab onto the ladder of the flatcar rolling our way. After you're on top of the deck, I'll toss the gear to ya.

Take caution though, space is limited inside this isle."

"Have no fear Bubba's here."

"That's what scares me."

My heart skipped a beat when his feet dragged the ground until he was able to secure them in the foot rung. Once on top of the deck, I trotted alongside the car and tossed the packs to him, then latched a hold.

We sat crossed legged on the deck and watched morning rush hour traffic inch along Interstate 5. The sun was already climbing up into a cloudless sky and it looked as though it were going to be another perfect spring day.

Bubba spotted two blondes, sitting in a white Ford Galaxy convertible with the top down, momentarily stopped in morning rush hour traffic. The girl on the passenger side happened to glance over toward the train. When she saw us sitting on the flatcar, she stood up on top of the passenger seat and hooted and hollered, giving us the thumbs up. Then the other girl shouted out something.

"Look!" Bubba said. "They're twins."

For some unknown reason he jumped up, whipped off his shirt, and performed muscle poses, as though he were Mr. Universe. Both of the girls went wild. The passenger stood back up on the seat and whistled loud enough, Bubba and I could hear her. Then he wolf whistled back loud enough to blow my eardrums out. We waved and shouted back and forth until our blonde babes vanished around a bend.

Shortly after, the train eased into the Tacoma switchyard and strings of railcars were on both sides of us.

We zigged zagged through a maze of railcars until we found a service road. Eventually, came upon an old building near the tracks. There was a tall man standing next to it who stood well over six feet tall, but couldn't have weighed more than a hundred and twenty pounds soaking wet. He was lanky, and sickly looking. His shaggy blond hair hung down in his eyes, with pieces of dried grass caught in it. He had a small oval mouth, high boney cheeks and long a narrow pointed nose, with pathetic flashing green eyes that reminded me of a sad homely puppy that nobody wanted. The man was wearing a red sweat stained tee shirt, loud yellow checked trousers, about four inches too short. Red argyle socks and brown beat up wingtip shoes set off this strange clamorous outfit.

"I'm Free Bird and this is Bubba Lee." I said, as I dropped my pack.

"Name's Andy," he said in an irritating, squeaky voice.

"Where are ya from?" I asked.?

Then Andy proceeded to tell us he was from Spokane, and that his wife had thrown him out, along with a lot more information neither of us really wanted to hear. As his depressing story unfolded Bubba, glanced over at me and rolled his eyes.

"We gotta get movin'," I said agitated.

"Where to?"

"We heard about a Catholic Church in the area that puts on a good lunch for the homeless."

"I know the place," he blurted. "Lunch is at 11:00. They'll give ya a bag of groceries if ya ask em'em."

"That'd be helpful to our cause. We still have a long road ahead of us. Do you want to tag along?"

"I don' think so, I'm in bad shape. Comin' down off a long drunk. Food don't sound too good."

"I guess we'll be moving on then. Take care."

Bubba and I climbed a steep winding staircase, up the side of a rock cliff to get to the downtown Tacoma city center. From there we followed Andy's instructions until we found ourselves standing at the bottom of a mammoth hill. Only then did I realize why he wasn't up to the task.

"Do we have to climb that?" Bubba groaned.

"Only if ya wanna' eat."

"Is it worth it?"

"Buck up and quit you're whining!"

Half way up the hill, we stopped to take a break.

"Those babes were smokin'', Bubba said," as he swiped his shirt sleeve across his forehead.

"They were a couple of lookers."

"I'd rather be in that convertible with them, instead of standing on this hillside sweating like a pig."

"That makes two of us. Come on stud muffin lets get this over with."

Shortly after we topped the hill, we saw a crowd of people standing outside of a large Catholic Church. We assumed we were in the right place so we sat down on the curb and waited. After the door opened we mingled our way into the line.

The lunch room was inside an expansive gymnasium, attached to the side of the church. Inside, was row after row of long banquet style tables, each with a large silver stainless steel bowl placed in the center, heaped with sandwiches? The smell of fresh soup and hungry voices filled the air. After served our bowls of steaming vegetable beef soup' we sat down at the nearest table with vacancy and commenced to slurping and chomping down on fresh bologna sandwiches.

"Eat until you're stuffed," I said. "It might be a while before we get a hot meal again."

"I plan on it," Bubba said, with his mouth full.

When neither of us could eat another bite, we asked an elderly gentleman, working on the soup line, how to go about getting some traveling groceries.

"Right over there in that room," he said pointing.

Inside the room was an attractive young lady sitting behind a desk, she looked to be in her twenties.

"Can I help you?" she said with a warm smile.

"Well," I stuttered, feeling self conscious of my ragged appearance. "I'm on my way down to California to find work." Can you help me out with some traveling groceries?"

"We can accommodate you," she said compassionately. "That's what we're here for. Sign your name on the roster."

I was hesitant, so I wrote down the name of a close friend of mine, Rick Swanson. She stooped over and picked up a grocery bag from the floor, then handed it to me. Then she pulled out a hunk of ring bologna from a large cooler, and stuffed it inside the bag.

"Good luck in California," she said, then took the next person in line.

When I stepped outside Bubba was sitting out on the curb.

When he saw me coming, he jumped up.

"What's inside the bag?" he asked excitedly.

I dumped its contents on the ground. To our surprise there was a variety of single serving cans of beanies and weenies, Chicken and dumplings, Vienna sausages, beef stew, and chicken noodle soup, twenty four and the pound of ring bologna, and a loaf of wheat bread? We divvied the goods between the packs and then we took off.

The smell of saltwater and fish rose to greet us. At the top of the hill we stopped to watch a fishing trawler chug across the sapphire blue harbor far below, with a flock of screeching seagulls hovering above.

"I don't know about you kid, but I'm ready to go to Wishram!"

"Let's got to Wishram," Bubba yelped.

Andy was still sitting where we had left him when we got back to the yard.

"Want something to eat?" I asked. "The church gave us plenty."

"Not now. I could sure use a smoke, but my hands are too shaky to roll one," he groaned.

"I'll try rolling a couple for ya, but there's no guarantee how well they'll turn out."

I managed to roll up four pregnant looking cigarettes. Afterward, I stuck put one between Andy's lips and lit it.

According to Buzz, our train wasn't due in for a couple more hours, so I started a fire and got coffee on.

About 3:00 o'clock we heard locomotives rumbling somewhere in the middle of the yard.

"What do ya say we gitty up on out of here?" I said excited.

"Let's go to Wishram!" shouted Bubba

Shortly after, we heard squeaky brakes followed by a loud pssst.

"They're picking up cars, giving us more time to find a ride!"

"Would it o.k. if I tag along?" asked Andy.

"If you're comin', let's go."

We hopped over a few vacant tracks, and then climbed over strings of cars, until we found the track our train was on. Then I had Bubba step around the other side of the lead car, from where the engines had broke away from the train. Andy and I walked together on the other side. Then we started to make our way toward the rear of the train.

We'd walked nearly the full length of the train when the cars jolted, followed hissing air lines.

"We're out of time," I said.

Seconds later the train eased forward. Hope of catching it seemed lost; until Bubba shouted over that he had spotted an open boxcar on his side. I boosted Andy up onto the cup-link, between the cars, instructing him to reach around to the other side and grab onto the ladder, then climb down, assuring him Bubba would help give him a lift on the other side. But he froze.

"I can't do it," he whined pathetically.

"It's your choice. Ether you do it, or I leave you standing out here looking like a fool. It's up to you. You think you're scared now. Wait until the train is screaming down the track at sixty plus miles an hour."

Finally he reached around and groped for the ladder. And then swung his leg around and scaled down the ladder, to the ground. This entire time the train was picking up speed.

"Hurry up, damn it, before you get us both killed."

I scaled down the ladder right behind him. Bubba gave him a lift up into the car, then I tossed him my pack and swung up inside.

"Yeah, we're on our way now," I shouted.

The mainline curved out at the head of the yard, and then ran out along the shore of Puget Sound.

Bubba and I sat in the doorway and gazed out at the lavish homes that were strung along the shoreline of the Sound.

South of Tacoma the train pulled off into a siding and stopped. There were no more homes along the shore, only a stretch of vacant beach as far as the eye could see. The bay was almost glass calm, except for a slight ripple that shimmered under the afternoon sun like millions of sparkling diamonds.

Bubba and I observed a young woman and two children walking along the edge of the water with a flock of screeching seagulls hovering above them. Periodically, the children stooped over and plucked seashells from the white sandy beach. Then they would drop them into the blue sand buckets clutched in their tiny hands.

Suddenly, the afternoon serenity was pierced by the horn blast of a car ferry steaming out toward the islands. The gypsy stirred deep within my soul and a chill ran down my spine, remembering why I loved the freedom of the road. The car lurched forward, we were underway once again.

After the train turned inland, we ran along the outer edge of Olympia. Later we rumbled through the towns of Centralia, and then Challis. The entire time since we'd departed from Tacoma, Andy sat hidden in the shadows at the rear of the car, smoking. Every so often, I'd glance back and see his face glow when taking a puff from his smoke.

South of Challis Bubba got bored and spread his bedroll out near the door and read. I figured that was as good a time as any to fish out my journal from my pack and make an entry. It had been a while since my last entry.

Bubba and I have successfully completed the first   leg of our journey, over the rugged Cascade Mountain Range. Our first night, on the road, we spent in a railroad switchyard, on the outskirts of Seattle, where we met an old hobo, named Buzz and his esteemed companion Bear.   After my near death encounter with his monster black, Newfoundland dog, "Bear," Buzz invited us into his camp and treated us like family. He fed us a hot meal fit for kings. There was a touch a magic in the air when he shared many tales with him and Bear rambling across the Nation by way of the steel rail. The memory of that night will forever be imprinted into my heart.   Though Society might label Buzz as nothing more than a lowly old hobo, I'll always remember him and Bear as the true items, gallant knights of the open road.

I set down the journal, stood up and poked my head out the door and took in deep breaths of the rich smells expelling from Mother Earth. Shadows grew long out across the land, as the sun arched over onto the western horizon. After the giant fireball plunged into a cloud line the evening sky exploded with the shades of brilliant pink, purple, crimson, and bright amber.

The sunset was only a fleeting glimmer on the horizon and stars had already begun to speckle the night sky when I woke the kid and helped him move his stuff to the front of the car. He immediately snuggled down inside his bedroll and fell back to sleep. I rolled out next to him and was almost asleep myself, when the flashing lights of a clanging railroad crossing zinged past the open door. Moments later the inside of the car flooded with light when oncoming locomotives screamed past. I sat back on my palms and watched the blurred railcars zing past. Then darkness swallowed the inside of the car again. The song "Born to be Wild," by Steppenwolf, reeled through my mind as I lay inside my cozy old sack: Clickety clack! Clickety, clack! Clickety clack!

Chapter 7

     I woke with a start. The train was sitting still. Outside a howling wind rocked and squeaked the coach. Yet, I could still hear Andy snoring like a rhino at the other end.

We must be in Vancouver, I thought, as I stretched. When I got up to check out our position, I realized that it was down right frigid inside the car. After I threw on my down coat, I blundered toward the almost invisible door. There were railcars on the next track over, telling me we were most definitely sitting in a switchyard. As much as I regretted to wake the kid, we had to get moving if we were to catch the Wishram train yet that night.

I nudged him, "Leave me alone," he groaned.

"Come on, we have a train to catch."

     "Alright! Alright! Alright! Is riding freight-trains always getting up in the middle of the night?" he growled.

     "That pretty much sums it up alright."

     He lay there a moment before coming around. "Shit, it's cold," he screeched when he sat up.

     "Where are we?" Andy asked sleepily.

"Nice going, loud mouth. I wanted to get outta' here without him."

"We're in Vancouver. The kid and I are gonna make our way down to the departure yard and try to catch out on the Wishram train. We're out of here as soon as we're packed."

Bubba scanned the perimeter one last time with the flashlight for anything we might have overlooked. Then we climbed down out of the car.

We hadn't got far down the track before Andy came running up behind us.

"Wait a minute," he gasped thru chattering teeth, wearing only a light spring jacket. "I'm goin with ya."

A canopy of black clouds loomed over the tops of the railcars and distant yard lights cast long ominous down the narrow corridor while we trudged toward the departure yard. And the brutal northwestern whistling down the alisle rocked and squeaked the railcars on both sides like a spook house at a carnival. Suddenly a flock of pigeons flew up right in front of us, so close, I felt the wind of wings flapping in my ears. All three of us screamed like little girls. when

"I've about had enough of this shit," growled Andy. "If we don't get out of this wind soon, it's gonna eat us alive."

"Why'd we even get out of bed?" Bubba grumbled."

"I've got an idea," I butted in.

"What?" they both said in unison.

"Why don't you two crybabies go crawl into a boxcar and go to bed, while make my way down to the departure yard and catch out on my Wishram train."

"We just might do that," Bubba snarled.

While we were arguing, Bubba happened to look up and noticed that we were standing beneath a bridge that spanned over the top of the yard.

"Look! He shouted. Someone is burning a fire at the other end.

Then it was a scramble to get to the fire. We had to climb over several strings of cars before we were close enough to see the fire. As far as we could tell there were only two men sitting on crates beside a roaring fire.

"I've got a bad feeling about these guys, I whispered. They look like a couple of hard core thugs."

By then Andy and Bubba had already hurtled the cup link and were running toward the fire like a couple of psychos. I had no other choice but to follow.

One of the men had a fat round face with only a couple of teeth remaining in his mouth and his eyes went off in different directions. He reminded me of a big fat jack O' lantern. As far as I could tell, the other man was tall and skinny with a bony face, and narrow shifty eyes. Both were wearing old dirty suit coats and greasy ragged dress pants that shinned under the firelight. They looked as though they hadn't bathed for quite some time. I estimated their age somewhere in their fifties.

"This is Bubba Lee out of Texas, and Andy, out of Washington, and I'm Freebird out of Michigan," I said.

"You a cita?' boy?" said pumpkin head.

"No sir," I answered.

"If ya wanta' sit by da' fire, just say so. Ya Don' hav' to act all proper and put on airs."

"I'm Floyd, and this here's Tommy."

There were a couple of other crates next the fire. But as I went to sit on one, Bubba hurried and beat me to it, while Andy sat on the other. So I sat on top of my pack to draw in the heat with my hands. I couldn't remember ever appreciating warmth as much as I did at that moment.

I panicked for a second when the last string of cars we had just climbed over jerked and rolled forward. But I knew that couldn't be our train.

While we were sitting around the fire, I couldn't help notice how Floyd kept eyeballing my pack in a way that made me feel uneasy. But that didn't rattle me as much as when both of them looked at each other as though a dastardly plan was hatching between two sinister minds. My gut feeling told me it was time to get the hell out of there. Buty by then old shifty eyes had already wrapped his arm around Bubba's neck with knife a held to his throat.

"Now ya boys listen real good, lay them packs down and all ya' mona', or the boy gits'cut."

Suddenly Andy sprung up and sprinted off into the shadows, like the coward I suspected he was.

"Ya tell him make him come back now, or I spill the boy's blood," Tommy growled, pressing his knife tighter against Bubba's throat.

"Don't you worry about him; he doesn't have any money anyway. He's just a coward," I said, attempting to sooth the man. "He's running scared with his tail between his legs. We'll give ya everything we have. Just don't hurt the kid", I pleaded.

But in my mind, I was already scheming on how we were going to get our stuff back. There were only two old men, both coming down off a bad drunk. I knew neither was thinking straight, only thinking out of desperation.

A couple minutes later, I spotted Andy out of the corner of my eye, creeping along the edge of the shadows with a two by four, about four feet long. He grinned when our eyes made contact. I shook my head no; terrified he'd only make matters worse. So I jumped up and tossed my wallet on the ground to divert their attention. Both men's eyes immediately were fixated upon it. Then Andy made his move and leaped into the ring of fire, wielding the board like a mad man. Somehow, he managed to smack Pumpkin head in the ribcage and he slumped over. Through all the commotion shifty eyes made the fatal mistake of taking his attention off the kid for only a split second. Suddenly Bubba's elbow flew up and smashed him in the nose. Blood splattered everywhere. Then Andy took a swing at Shifty eyes, but he managed to duck in the nick of time, as the board grazed just over the hairs of his head. Then Bubba stepped back and dropped kicked Shifty eyes square in the gonads. Then he let out a god awful howl. Then Bubba went into a rage and repeatedly kicked the man in his ribs. By then Pumpkin head was coming back around. I ran over and kicked him in the gut. He doubled over. Bubba was still kicking the poor man in the ribs.

"Calm down, before you kill him." I shouted. Then I literally picked the kid up by the waist, his with his feet still kicking.

"Let's grab our gear." I yelled, and make a run for that slow moving train a track over."

We snatched our gear and then ran for the train. Bubba turned around and kicked shifty eyes one last time in his ribs.

"That'll teach ya to put a knife to my throat you son of a bitch." Then he turned and ran over to the train.

The only cars rolling past at the time were Gondola's full of scrap steel. After we latched onto the nearest car, we scaled the ladder behind each other. The edges of the scrap steel were so razor sharp, we were forced to sit on the top edge of the car.

When our car rolled out onto the railroad trestle that divided Oregon from Washington. Aa bitter northeastern howled down the Columbia River with a vengeance, spitting a cold rain, as though it were literally trying to pluck us off each one of us, off the edge of the car, and hurl us down into the black frigid waters below. We just bowed our heads, gritted our teeth and took it like men.

A couple minutes later the train rolled into the Portland, Oregon Union Pacific switchyard. I freaked out, because I had heard too many horror stories about the U. P. dicks, in that yard, giving out ninety day sentences in the clinker for trespassing on railroad property. But we had no other choice but to ride it out, because we were all soaked to the bone by then. I knew if we didn't make a fire soon, we'd be in peril of slipping into hypothermic shock.

After the train stopped, we jumped down and started trudging through dreary, dripping corridors until we found a service road. We were afraid to walk directly on it, so we walked up near the cars. A few hundred yards down, we came upon a grove of trees off to the side. We plunged into them and started looking for anything that could possibly burn. We tried every trick we knew to get the wet wood to ignite with no avail. The situation was bleak until I remembered something that an old Native American friend of mine had told me a while back. He said that if I were to ever have trouble getting a fire started, I should search for a fallen tree, because the sap at the tree's base coats the wood, protecting it from moisture. I fished out my flashlight and small hatchet from my pack, then ran into the trees in search of the nearest fallen tree. The first one I came to, I chopped off a handful of splinters from the base. When I got back, I had Andy and Bubba huddle around me to shield the wind, while attempting to ignite the splinters, but my hands trembled so bad, it was tough to hold the match steady. On the third try, the slivers slowly started to ignite. Ever so gently I fed the precious shards into the fragile flames until a small fire began to slowly take off. Then I told Bubba where the tree was, and how to chop off more shards. Minutes later, he returned with both of his hands full of splinters. We continued to worship the flames, desperately trying to extract every ounce of heat we could from them.

From out of nowhere, headlights came straight for us. Then the Ford Bronco was sliding sideways, straight toward us, spraying gravel. When the vehicle came to rest, a heavyset man flung open the door and did a spread eagle across the hood, with pistol in hand, barking orders for us to lie down on our stomachs and to keep our hands where he could see them. Moments later a pickup truck pulled in behind the Bronco. Two men got out and stood behind the detective. The dick then ordered us not to move a muscle, or suffer sudden death, while the other two rifled through our belongings. They literally dumped everything out of our packs, onto the muddy wet ground. Then they searched through our bedrolls. Afterwards, they deliberately tossed them into the mud. Eventually, we were ordered to stand up one at a time and assume the position, while they frisked us. Once the detective was satisfied we were not a threat, he ordered us to stand at ease.

"From Michigan," he growled, while looking at my driver's license with his flashlight. What the hell are you doing in my yard boy?"

"Actually, we didn't mean to enter your yard sir."

"You're here ain't you?

"Actually we got on the wrong train, in the Vancouver yard."

"That don't fly with me, boy!" He grunted. Then he glared at Bubba. What are you doing with this kid? He doesn't even have identification. The way I see it, you're in a heap of trouble son."

My heart dropped down into my stomach. We were screwed. Andy and I were going to jail. And God only knew what was going to happen to the kid. *Come on Lord you asked me to take the kid home,* I prayed silently in desperation, *we could use some help about now.*

Out of the blue, the detective had a change of heart.

"You get your shit together and get your sorry asses the hell out of my yard before I change my mind," he yelled.

That was good enough for me. He didn't need to say it twice. We ran around like chickens with our heads cut off, plucking our belongings off the wet ground. When we had everything picked up, the angry detective pointed to a hill and ordered us to start climbing.

"If you ever dare to venture into my yard again, you'll be locked up until hell freezes over," he barked.

I didn't know about the others, but I had no intention of coming back anytime in the near future.

The hillside was muddy wet clay. We slipped and fell a few times before reaching the top. On the other side of the hills base there was as an interstate. None of us had a clue to which interstate it was, or even what direction it was going. We slid most of the way down on our rumps. Afterwards, we sat alongside the highway and scraped as much clay from the soles of our shoes as we could, and off the back of our britches before moving on. Down the road a piece we ducked under an overpass bridge for shelter. Beneath the bridge was a cement ledge at the top of the embankment. The ledge was about four feet wide, perfect to crash on if we rolled out head to toe. The cover of the bridge broke most of the wind. After we rolled out the bedrolls, we found that they weren't as bad off as we feared, only wet in spots. The howling northeastern sang a sad eerie refrain through the rafters of the bridge.

Throughout the night I'd periodically, startle awake, then drift back into a restless sleep.

CHAPTER 8

Traffic was rolling along at a steady flow the next time I woke, yet it was still dark as night. But the volume of vehicles zooming past below told me it had to be morning. I was sore and miserable, and felt as though I hadn't slept a wink. It was going to be a long day.

By the time we pulled ourselves together, traffic was practically bumper to bumper.

"No one's gonna stop to pick us up," grumbled Andy. "We look like hammered shit!"

"We need a plan," chimed Bubba.

"Whatcha got in mind kid?"

"What if I clean up as best I can, then walk up against traffic a couple hundred yards? Then I'll turn around to start hitchin'? When somebody stops, which they will, because I'm so handsome, I'll coax them into picking you guys up."

"Spoken like a true Texan. What if they won't stop? How will I find you when I don't even know what highway were on, your Lordship? I don't feel good about it, but our options are minimal. Andy's right, we're gonna have a tough time getting out of here."

The kid combed his hair and washed his face with the little water we had left. Then he squared his shoulders and proceeded to march off.

"I don't know about this," I said, vexed.

"If he don't do it, chances of gettin' out of here ain't good."

"I bet we look pretty ragged to these people zipping past in their vehicles."

Bubba walked down the road about a quarter of mile, then he turned around and started hitching.

Andy and I were facing away from traffic to shield the wind and didn't notice the red pickup truck that had pulled over off on the shoulder of the road behind us.

"Jump in the back," we heard Bubba shouting. He was standing outside the truck waving us over. The driver was a middle aged African American. We grabbed our stuff and ran. We no more thaen tossed our gear into the back, and hopped over, when the truck zoomed out into morning traffic.

Even with our backs against the window of the cab, our teeth chattered like Morse -code, as the bitter wind swirled around us. I turned around and knocked on the back window and asked Bubba to inquire what interstate we were on, and how far the man was going"

When he opened the back window of the cab warm air gushed through the opening. "We're on Interstate 5, headed south. He's going as far as Eugene."

"Eugene's over a hundred miles south of Portland, I yelled over the wind. From there we can catch a southbound, Southern Pacific and take it all the way down to Roseville, California.

"Your plan actually worked like a charm," kid."

He closed the window wearing an ear to ear grin.

"Andy, once we get to Eugene, we'll find the nearest Laundromat and wash and dry everything we own. From Eugene we'll hook a southbound and ride it all the way down into sunny California."

"That sounds like a plan to me," he said through chattering teeth.

Every few minutes Bubba would turn around and flash us a cocky grin, as to say, while you chumps are in the back freezing, I'm up here in this warm toasty cab. I rapped on the window to get his attention. When he turned back around, I smacked my fist into my hand to let him know he was in for it when go to Eugene. He abruptly turned back around with a worried look. Before I turned around, I looked down the highway through the windshield and saw what looked to be the end of the cloudbank.

A few minutes later we rolled out from beneath the black canopy of clouds, into pure unadulterated sunshine. As we pulled away from the clouds the events that took place back in Portland only seemed like something from a distant nightmare. Except for the clouds fading in the distance, there wasn't another in sight. The sun felt like heaven as it warmed our chilled bones.

When the man dropped us off on a downtown Eugene exit ramp, the three of us walked up to the driver window and thanked him for helping us out of bad situation.

When the truck was out of sight, Andy and I chased Bubba round until we caught him. While Andy held him down, I gave him a knuckle rub from hell. Andy topped it with a few slugs in the arms. Bubba laughed the entire time. Satisfied with our revenge, on the little pecker woodpeckerwood, we gathered our stuff and headed out to find the nearest Laundromat. This little venture was gonna put a good dent in the little money I had left, but it needed to be done. Everything we owned was either damp, muddy or both. There was so much rainfall in that part of the country, it was vital to keep your belongings dry, or suffer the fate of mold and mildew.

We found a coin operated laundry a few blocks off the highway with giant size washers. We stuffed the three sleeping-bags, our coats, and our canvas packs; we had dismantled from their frames, into a single giant size washer. Everything else went into a small machine.

While waiting for our clothes to get done I leafed through an outdated Field and Stream magazine, Bubba read a Louis L' Amour book and Andy paced nervously when he wasn't outside having a smoke.

After operation laundry was completed, we took off to find the local Salvation Army Thrift store. I had made up my mind then and there, if Andy was traveling with us, the high water britches had to go.

There's nothing like a good hard luck story to soften the heart of a woman. We finagled the lady working the store, to sell us a backpack, winter coat, two pairs of jeans, flannel shirt, and a decent pair of walking shoes, for less than eight bucks, because I told her it was all the money we had in the world between us.

We almost didn't recognize Andy when he walked out of the dressing room, wearing his new duds. I have to admit, he seemed almost happy for the moment, which was unusual for him.

"We've got one thing left to do," I said. We need to go to the mission and get some hot showers before we blow this town. With some luck, we might even catch out on a southbound before the sun sets."

"Let's go to California!" squealed Bubba.

"I'm all for California," Andy agreed.

Andy chattered practically non stop most of the way to the mission. But Bubba didn't say much of anything. He did, however, manage to wolf whistle a couple of college babes, wearing short shorts and low cut halter tops. They beamed wide smiles, waved and then put a little more jiggle into their wiggle.

I had Bubba walk up to the door with me when we arrived at the mission, in the hope, whoever answered might have sympathy, because we had a kid with us. We knocked a couple of times, but no answer. We were about to walk away, when the door partially opened and an elderly man poked his head out.

"What do you want?" he growled in a flinty voice.

"We need showers desperately," I said with all the humbleness I could muster.

"Does this look like a motel to you!" he growled. "The answer is no!"

Just before the old timer slammed the door, Bubba's eyes and his met. Then he reopened the door.

"Hold on, fellas," he said. "It's too late to do anything for you today, but if you come back tomorrow morning, say around eight, the bosses will be gone. Then I'll see what I can do, unless you're interested in checking into the mission for the night."

"No thanks, we prefer to sleep outside. We'll be back in the morning."

"By any chance, you boys looking for a place to crash?"

"Maybe," I said. "Why?"

"I might be inclined to tell you about my secret place, if you all give me your word you won't say anything about it to anyone else."

"We swear!" we said all at the same time and made a pact we'd never tell, even if we were tortured, or worse. That made the old guy break a smile, in turn, he gave us directions on how to get to his sacred place that was supposedly magical.

"You boys have been riding trains, haven't you?"

I was reluctant to say anything, but felt he could be trusted.

"It shows that much," I laughed?.

"I'm George," he said, as he extended his calloused hand to shake. "I know a hobo when I see one. Been riding near thirty years now. Started when I in my twenties, been ever since. Once the clickety clack gets into your blood, it's near impossible to quit. I'd sure appreciate it, if you boys would pick me up a pouch of tobacco, and rolling papers, in the morning."

"Consider it done!" I said

"Well duty calls boys. I'll see you in the morning." Then he shut the door.

"I guess there's been a change of plan. We're not going anywhere today. To tell you the truth, I think we could use a good night's sleep on solid ground. I hope this sacred tree is as wonderful as the old timer claims.

"Another delay," Bubba said frustrated.

"Hang in there kid, we'll get there."

George's sacred tree was supposed to be past a public park, and off a bicycle path about twenty feet, give or take.

While walking through the park near where our camp was supposed to be located, we sat on a park bench and watched eight guys play basketball on an outside court. They were aggressive well-oiled machines. All of them managed to pull off some amazing shots. I wondered if they weren't college ball players blowing off some steam. We got so engrossed into their game, we didn't realize it was getting dark, and that it had begun to sprinkle.

"I guess we'd better get moving," I said.

"Do we have to?" Bubba whined

"It's getting dark and sprinkling. We need to find this place while we can still see."

"Your right," agreed Andy.

"What are we waiting for," said Bubba.

Not far past the park, we walked down the jogging path. Before long we were standing in front of a massive old pine tree, just off a jogging trail about twenty feet, and exactly where George said it would be. The large tree's thick boughs sloped almost down almost to the ground, forcing us to crawl under on our stomachs. Once beneath the old tree, the lowest branches on its trunk were high enough for Bubba to stand up straight without bumping his head. They also created about an eight foot diameter from the trees base.

"This is totally bitchin'," Bubba said excitedly.

"It is pretty neat," agreed Andy.

Standing beneath the realm of the old relic reminded me of a Native American teepee with a trunk in the center. Before long the intoxicating scent of pine needles made us feel drowsy. Then my arms and legs felt like lead. Suddenly I could no longer keep my eyes open. We didn't waste anytime rolling out our bedrolls onto the lofty bed of scented pine needles that had accumulated through countless years. Burrowing down into my fresh clean bedroll made the experience even more alluring.

"George was right," I said yawning. "This old tree does have a touch of magic."

Bubba popped up and gasped, "We're not goin' to Wishram are we?"

"I'm afraid not. I wanted to take you there more than anything in the world," I mumbled. That was my last thought before the steady rhythm of the pitter patter of rain took me down into peaceful dreams.

Chapter 9

The rhythmic cooing of mourning doves serenaded me awake. I sat up, yawned and stretched. It had been quite some time since I could remember feeling so refreshed and rested. It was still dark beneath the tree and I wanted to sleep longer, but Mother Nature called. So I put on a pair of shorts and a tee shirt. Then I slipped out from beneath the canopy.   Shafts of sun light sliced through the misty morning haze and the fragrance of flower blossoms scented the morning air and countless birds chattered in the surrounding trees. Walking on the dew drenched grass felt soothing between my toes. Regardless of the wet ground, I sat down to try and drink in the morning serenity, until joggers and bicyclists began to amble on past, by the dozens, out on the path. Then it was time to roust the boys. I crawled back under and nudged Bubba.

"I was dreaming about an old girlfriend, back in Texas," he yawned, until you woke me and ruined the best part."

"Your dream girl will have to wait until' tonight, we have big day ahead of us, get a move on."

"One more wink, he said.

Andy and I were up and packed before Bubba came up for air again.

We blinked under the morning sun after crawling from beneath the canopy of branches.   As we walked away, I looked back, knowing I'd return again someday to the mystical old tree.

On the way to the mission we made a pit stop at a convenient mart.   There I picked up a couple pouches of Bull Durham, a quart of chocolate milk, and two packs of Hostess Suzie Qs. We consumed them and the chocolate milk out on the curb.

"That was the breakfast of champions," Bubba said, rubbing his belly.

"It hit the spot," agreed Andy.

Most of the way to the mission, Bubba rambled on relentlessly about his dream girl back in Texas. However, I managed to tune most of it out. My thoughts were primarily focused on getting back on the rail, and then on into California.

Upon are arrival at the mission, George opened the door and whisked us inside, putting his finger to his mouth to be quiet while we slipped through the darkened kitchen. Andy and Bubba took off for the showers, but I stopped and handed George the rolling papers and a pouch of tobacco.

"God bless you, son," he said. "What'd you guys think of my secret spot?"

"It was really something. In all my travels, I haven't ever jungled at a finer place. I believe there really is a touch of magic under that old tree.

I told you. Found it a few years' back. And been goin' there ever since.

"It's none of my business. But what are you doing traveling with that young kid? Don't you that you could get into a lot of trouble having him with you."

"I know. But he's homeless. I found him destitute in a mission back in Yakima. He's been thrown out of his own mother's house by her abusive alcoholic boyfriend. From what I heard, it was a pretty bad situation there. I'm just trying to get him back home to where his dad lives in Dallas, Texas. That's why we didn't want to stay at the mission. We were afraid to show identification, if you know what I mean."

I suspected as much. If that the case, it's a good thing you're doing for the kid then. It's getting crazy out on the tracks anymore. Too damn many nut cases. Please take good care of him then."

"I'll guard him with my life," I promise."

"You're a good boy," he said. "I can tell if people are good or not. You best get into the shower before the boss comes back and we're all in deep shit."

"Yes sir."

In the time it took us to shower, George had made up six sandwiches and filled a paper bag full of fresh fruit, and refilled our water jug. Then he gave us directions on what track our train would most likely be made up on, and precisely where to catch it in the yard.

We thanked George many times outside on the back stoop and said our farewells.

"I'd better get back to work boys," he said slightly choked up. Maybe our paths will cross again someday?"

"I'll be looking forward to it," I said , just before the door shut.

When we left the mission, the sun was already up in a cloudless sky and the fresh scent of flower blossoms still perfumed the morning breeze.

It'd been quite some time since I had been in the Eugene yard. But thanks to George's directions, on where we should cut in from the street, and what track our train would most likely be made up on, we managed to keep on the straight and narrow. After we cut into the yard we began counting tracks, while weaving through the narrow corridors and climbing over rows of railcars. Before long we found a train already made up on the track number George estimated. Where we came out at, we were only a few cars from the front of the train. But the power wasn't even hooked up yet. We looked up that way and didn't see anything open, so Andy climbed over to the other side, while Bubba and stayed together and started walking toward the rear of the train.

We walked better than a mile before taking a break. Then we sat down on the gravel and chatted beneath a railcar.

"Does this son -of -a bitch even have an end to it," Andy grumbled.

It's a long one, I won't argue that. We have to be close to the end by now," I said.

"I hope so," Andy retorted.

"Amen to that," the kid agreed.

About twenty cars down the line, after our break, Andy and I found ourselves gawking at each other through opposing doors. Both sides were wide open on the old Southern Pacific boxcar. I tossed my pack in, and swung up. Then I walked over to the other side to give Andy a lift. That's when I noticed two men that were sprawled out on the ground, between the railcars, both with a bottle of booze in their hand.

"There ain't no more open cars," said a huge fat man. "I know because me and Montana walked this whole damn train. And it's a long sonbitch' let me tell ya. So if yer planin' on ridien' this here train, yer' gonna have to do it with us. We was told it's goin' all the way to North Platte Nebraskee'."

"If we cut across the mountains," I said excited, "we can slice our time in half. Things are finally falling into place."

My theory of avoiding the higher mountain passes seemed to go right out the window. All I could think about then, was getting the kid home, with some luck, and still have time to double back to Lodi, before the cherry season was completely over.

"Kid, what do ya say we ride this train as far as Cheyenne, Wyoming?

From there, we'll catch a southbound Burlington Northern and work our way down into the big D."

"Yeah!" He yelled. "Let's go home!"

Along about then a breeze swirled through the boxcar with the nasty stench of body odor, so offensive, my nostrils burned like ammonia.

"One of those guys smells like something dead," I whispered.

"I can smell it too," Bubba said, covering his nose and gagging. The stench was so putrid, I considered catching another train, but the kid would have been heart broken. Andy quickly jumped back down and introduced himself, most likely, because they had booze.

"I'm Sheepherder," the fat man slurred, extending his filthy hand toward Andy. Then Sheepherder said he'd been tending sheep somewhere in Utah for the last six months, without ever coming into town once. I suspected most of the stench was coming from him.

"They call me Montana Red when they ain't mad at me," slurred the other man. Montana was a tall lanky man, wearing a cowboy hat, with a read bandana around his neck. He looked like a tall Texas cowboy. His face was beet red and his nose was pitted from years of drinking.

I wasn't overly anxious to befriend these guys. I didn't know them, and I sure as hell didn't trust em'em. Yet they were more than happy to share with Andy.

Strewn about the interior of the car were pieces of cardboard about a foot thick, and three feet wide and seven feet long. Most likely, they had been used for support for the prior load. I dragged a couple sheets to the front of the car, and then Bubba and I rolled out our bedrolls on top of them.

"These will keep us off the cold floor, while going over the hump."

I nagged the three relentlessly to get inside the boxcar. If any railroad workers were come along, all of us would have been in trouble. Finally they agreed that that might be best.

It was quite the ordeal for Sheepherder to pull his massive body up from ground level. When he stood up his enormous belly heaved up and down. Between the two, they only had a large Samsonite suitcase, and two ragged looking bedrolls.

It was even more of a fiasco to get Sheep Herder up inside the car. Montana slung his mammoth body up onto the deck, while Bubba and I tugged on his short chubby arms, gagging at the same time. Finally Montana was able to roll Sheepherder's huge torso onto the floor. The polka song "Roll out the Barrel" came to mind.

Once they were situated at the other end of the car, they all commenced to pouring down the booze like no tomorrow. Andy's eyes almost popped out of their sockets when Sheepherder opened up the huge Samsonite suitcase to grab another bottle. Its entire contents consisted of nothing but bottles of liquor. There wasn't a single stitch of clothing inside the case. This didn't sit well with me at all. Trouble was the last thing we needed.

The kid was so hyped to get underway, he was making me crazy. I pleaded with him to read, but he said that he was too excited to concentrate.

A couple of hours later we finally heard air feeding into the lines, followed by the chain reaction of banging cars. Bubba ran over to a door and spouted out the railroad logos on the sides of the railcars as the train eased out of the yard.

Once out on the mainline, I stood back in the door a ways and watched the houses and railroad crossings zing past.

Bubba, shouted out to a crowd of people standing outside the Amtrak railroad depot. Most of them waved back.

There couldn't be more of a perfect day to take a ride over the hump, I thought as I gazed out toward the snowcapped Cascades erected against a blue cloudless backdrop.

South of Eugene we began the climb into the foothills. As the long train wound around the sharp curves, I was able to see that there were, in fact, no other open cars on the entire its entire length that was well over a mile and half long.

"Look!" Bubba shouted, "There are three engines in the center, two more behind the caboose, and five pulling on the front."

"The extra engines are to help push us over the hump, because they're pulling some heavy duty tonnage," I explained.

"Bitchin!"

In the mountains, lush green grass and the brilliant colors of blossoming wild flowers carpeted the meadows and valley walls.

"Look Bubba!" said, pointing. "There's a herd of deer standing next to that pond." A snowcapped mountain peak and blues skies reflected upon the pool's glassed surface. Just then five locomotives of an oncoming train screamed past the open door. The railcars of the opposing train were so close; I could almost reach out and touch them. When the caboose ambled past there was the most beautiful woman I had ever seen standing on the back platform. Her long braided black hair that hung down to the middle of her back shimmered under the afternoon sun. And her piercing dark round eyes sent a jolt of electricity down my spine. She had high cheekbones and cocoa colored skin, and brazen thick, muscular brazen thighs. She was wearing khaki shorts, hiking boots and a red halter top. When our eyes met, they locked onto to each other's; in a way that made me feel as though we had both been searching our entire lives for each other. I clutched the side of the car and craned my neck until I almost fell out, trying desperately to stay locked upon her gaze, until my brazen beauty vanished around the bend.

"Yaw hoo," I shouted down the canyon.

North of Klamath Falls the train pulled into a siding. From the boxcar door was a majestic view of the renowned Crater Lake. Up until then, I'd only seen it in pictures. I had always wanted to go and check it out sometime, but never seemed to got around to it yet. The surrounding landscape reflected upon the sapphire mirror surface exactly the way, I had seen on numerous postcards. How I wanted to jump off the train and jungle out there for a couple of days and do some hiking and exploring. Unfortunately, I was under a binding contract with the Almighty himself. The car jerked forward, we were underway once again.

CHAPTER 10

I woke to the serenade of the three stooges snoring and farting at the other end of the car, loud enough to awake the dead. The train was sitting still. As much as I desired to stay snug in my bedroll, Mother Nature called. So I jumped up and stumbled toward the door. Railcars were on both sides of us so I assumed we were sitting in the K Falls yard. I was tempted to wake the kid and grab another train, but I would have never heard the end of it. With regret, I decided to stick it out. Besides, up until then we had made good time. I took care of business, and then crawled back in to the warmth of my old down sack, not giving the matter much more thought. I even smiled within when the train pulled out of the yard; confident the rest of our journey was going to be smooth sailing.

Several times during the night, I'd jerk awake and every time the train was stopped. Then I'd roll back over and fall off into a restless sleep again. The next time I woke, I reached for the water jug. As my eyes focused, I thought how it looked lopsided. When went to pick it up, I discovered that it was frozen solid. Everybody was standing over me with blue lips and chattering teeth, glaring down at my bedroll. Suddenly it dawned on me that mine was the only one made for temperatures below 32 degrees. I also noticed all the bolt heads on the car were frosted.

"We've been sittin' on top of this here on top of this here mountin' for damn near fer' hours now," Sheepherder groaned through clicking teeth.

Bubba was the only person I'd consider to let crawl inside my bedroll. As far as I was concerned, the others were shit out of luck. Then Sheepherder and Montana started arguing if they should take the chance of jumping down out of the car and starting a fire. The school of hard knocks had taught me long before, how fast a train could get rolling. I didn't want Bubba to have any part of it. So I jumped up and told him crawl inside my bedroll.

"Since we blew outta' the falls, dern' near nine hours ago," blubbered Sheepherder; "this train ain't even made it to Alturas, the first crew change."

"Are you sure we didn't sleep through it?" I said shocked.

"I know exactly where we are. We didn't."

"I think our best bet is to git' off this milk train from hell when it changes crews in Alturas," said Montana. "I don't know about anybody else, but I'm starting a fire."

Montana and Andy jumped down out of the car and scrounged around for anything that might burn. A few minutes later we hoisted Sheepherder down.

"If the train starts moving," I said, "and you can't get Sheepherder back on in time; I'll toss you your gear."

I knew if it were to start rolling, chances of getting him back on in time would be slim to none without someone getting hurt. When a boxcar is in a yard it's much easier to climb inside, because the tracks are at ground level. But out on the mainline, there's at least a foot of ballast beneath them, making it much tougher to get back in when the car is moving.

Bubba popped up. "You mean we're not goin to Cheyenne?"

"Montana's right, we're on the milk train from hell. We need to cut our losses and get off in Alturas. From there we'll catch the first westbound back into the falls.

Suddenly the profanities rolled off the end of his tongue like filth from a wet weather stream.

"These are your options," I growled. "Stay with the train and ride it to Cheyenne. From there guess your way home, if you don't freeze to death first. Or go back to the falls and go south, end of discussion. Make up your mind. Otherwise keep your mouth shut."

He mumbled something under his breath, then tunneled back down inside the bag and didn't say another word. I was so fuming mad, that I was afraid I'd lose my cool if he pursued the matter further. I didn't like snapping at him like that, but I had had my belly full of his cocky attitude.

With a little help from Jose Cuervo, the guys were able to get a fire started. However, only a few minutes later the air lines sang out.

"Fellas, I'm afraid that's your call."

It was a blessing that we were able to yank Sheepherder back inside the car before the train began to roll. Andy and Montana actually had to swing back inside while on the move.

When the train rolled into Alturas, Bubba and I cheered and high fived.

All of us were more than ready to get the hell out of that rolling icebox.

We were all in much better spirits after we had a fire going. However, the kid I weren't able to make coffee because our water was frozen solid. Even the can goods were frozen. But we were able to thaw a couple of them over the fire. I asked the others if they were hungry, but they declined. They were more interested in drinking. This business of drinking out in the open didn't sit well with me at all. I had made up my mind, then and there, as soon as we rolled back into to Klamath Falls, the kid and I, were going our own way.

It was at least a couple hours before we heard a westbound whistle beckoning us in the distance. As much as I hated backtracking, I figured if we sat on top of that mountain much longer, somebody could have easily froze to death. I was confident rerouting back through the Klamath was the right thing to do.

Apparently Montana had been to Alturas before. Where we'd made the fire was supposedly near to where the center of the train would be after it stopped to change crews

A few minutes later three Southern Pacific locomotives rumbled past. Bubba waved at the engineer. He in turn waved back out the small cockpit window. I was relieved that the knuckleheads had enough sense to hide the booze before the engines were in sight. Once the train had stopped, there was an open Burlington Northern boxcar only a couple of hundred yards up from us. We grabbed our gear and ambled that way.

Once operation Sheepherder was accomplished, the kid and I rolled out in the front of the car. The others settled in at the other end.

Bubba and I stood in the doorway and watched until Alturas faded around the bend.

CHAPTER 11

When we rolled back into Klamath Falls, I woke the kid and told him to get his things together, we were out of there. It was my hope to make our escape before the others woke. But when the engines broke air, the loud pssst woke Andy. He in turn rousted the twins. All three sat up and moaned and groaned. At least they were semi sober to the point they were somewhat functional. Immediately, Andy began to blubber that he needed to find a phone so he could call his wife. He had had enough of riding nasty old freight trains. He even swore he'd never drink again, if she'd only take him back and give him another chance.

"All I want to do is go home to my wife and straighten my life out," he blubbered. I wanted to say good riddance, but we at the least owed him our allegiance for coming back for us in Vancouver.

"If that's what you want," I forced myself to say, "Bubba and I will walk you to the depot and give you a proper goodbye."

Then Montana and Sheepherder decided they should go and say farewell to Andy too.

We threaded through a labyrinth of railcars, until we came out across from a small café near the tracks. Outside the facility was a lighted payphone. By then poor Sheepherder was drenched in sweat. We had to stop and wait until his mammoth belly quit heaving up and down. Then we walked out across open tracks. At the payphone Andy flashed me his puppy dog eyes, saying he needed the money to make the phone call. I dug into my pocket and literally slammed the coins into his hands.

"Here!" I said through clinched teeth.

From the moment Andy's wife answered he blubbered so pathetically that I wanted to reach over and bitch slap him. He carried on and on about how he was a changed man and even swore he'd never drink again if she'd only take him back. From what I could hear, it sounded as though she were crying also. After Andy had hung up, he said that she missed him, and wanted him back home as soon as possible. And that she was wiring him the money for a greyhound bus ticket as soon as she scraped up the cash.

On the way to the depot, Montana and Sheepherder insisted we walk through downtown Klamath Falls. To this day I have no idea why I agreed to their insane gjestuere that was a sure recipe for disaster.

People driving past, gawked and pointed at us as though we were a freak show at the circus. I felt like crawling underneath a rock. By then, I just wanted to get Andy to the depot, say good riddance, and then the kid and I would finally be free of the madness.

On the main street in downtown, Klamath Falls Sheepherder happened to spot a woman sitting in a parked car, next to the sidewalk, who was holding an infant in her lap. He immediately set down the big Samsonite suitcase and ran over to the open window of the vehicle and began making god awful goo, goo, gaa, gaa noises at the toddler. Instantly the baby's shrill cry echoed down the street and off buildings like an explosion. From out of nowhere, two police cruisers came to a screeching halt next to us. Then a cop jumped out from each vehicle, both shouting for us to lie down on the sidewalk, and keep our hands where they could see them. Bubba giggled through the entire event. I told him shut his mouth and do what he was told. I assumed we were in big trouble this time. When they found out the kid had no I.D, our journey would come to an abrupt end. I hate to ask you again Lord, but as you can see, we are in a jam once again and could use a little help about now, I mumbled to myself.

We were cuffed, and then instructed to stand up. Afterwards we were tucked into the police cruisers. They hadn't asked for identification yet. I assumed that would be done while being booked down at the station.

Bubba, Andy and I were jammed into the backseat of one of the cruisers, and Montana and Sheepherder in the other. I swear the springs sagged almost to the ground when Sheepherder sat down in the back of the other cruiser. I was awed they were even able to get the two of them in the back seat at the same time. The officer in their car immediately rolled down the window and covered his nose. Then he turned around and said something nasty to Sheepherder. Bubba wasere snickering. Our officer turned around and glared at us.

"What's so damn funny?" he snarled. Just then the voice of the other cop broke over the radio.

"I say we drop these lowlife scumbags off down to the rail yard and be rid of em'em. They're not even worth wasting our time on."

"I agree, over," our officer answered.

A few minutes we pulled up next to the Southern Pacific switchyard. After we were unloaded, they removed the cuffs and then popped the trunks, and handed us our gear. Then they sternly reprimanded us low life scumbags to be on the first train blowing smoke out of there town, because our kind wasn't wanted there. And if they ever saw us again, we'd wish we'd never been born.

"Take a bath fat boy," the other cop snarled at Sheepherder. "It'll take me a month get your stench out of my cruiser."

They glared at us with the meanest looks they could muster, then jumped into their cruisers and sped away, spraying gravel all over us.

I grabbed the kid by the arm: Come on we're outta' here. We're hanging out in the yard until a southbound rolls in.

"I've got to try and sneak over to that depot and catch my bus," Andy said. "I'm goin' home hell or high water."

"At least it's dark," I said. "I think you'll be o.k. if you stick to the back streets and keep clear of the street lights."

"Thanks for coming back for us back in Vancouver," Bubba said. "That took some real balls."

Andy actually started to choke up: "You're not so bad kid." Then he ruffled his curly locks. "Stay out of trouble kid." Then he turned and vanished into the night.

Bubba and I said our farewells to Montana and Sheepherder,; then we slinked off into the shadows of the yard.

We crawled inside an open boxcar next to the mainline for a vantage point of the activity in the yard.

Time seemed to stand still while sitting inside the darkened boxcar. We had no idea when the next southbound was due in. It could be a few minutes, or a few hours, meaning we could not afford the luxury of getting too comfy. After what seemed like hours later, Bubba broke the silence.

"How long do you think we've been sitting in here, " he whispered?

"Too long."

"My stomach has been growling ever since we've been here."

"Hah, what else is new, your stomach is always growling."

"But I ''m hungry myself. What do ya say we sneak over to that little café where Andy called his old lady and grab some grub to go?" Then we'll come back here and pig out."

"That's what I'm talking about," He said, rubbing his belly. "I'm so hungry I could eat the ass end of a steer."

"That's so Texas of you. I swear, you're stomach is an open pit, . aAnnd keep you're voice down!."

We stayed hidden in shadows of the yard until we were standing across from the café. I scanned up and down the track to make sure all was clear, then we dashed across to the café.

I was uneasy about leaving our packs outside the diner. Hopefully we weren't gonna be there too long to worry about it. All the tables were occupied until two men vacated a booth. We lunged for the open booth and scooted in before anyone else could. Before long, a pretty, tall waitress, with long legs, and curly blonde hair bouncing on her shoulders, pranced over to our table. She was wearing a low cut blouse and a pushup bra, displaying an eye full of cleavage. She had a nice pair and wasn't ashamed to let others know it.

"What'll it be, boys?" she said in a sexy seductive voice, while beaming us a sweet smile.

"A couple of cheese burgers, fries and two Cokes to go," I stammered.

"Anything else?"

Yeah, you to go, I thought. "That should do it. Oh, put a rush on that please. We're in a hurry."

"Ok boys," she said. As she bounced away, she turned her head back over her shoulder, flipped her curly blond hair and batted her baby blues in such a, I almost fell out of the booth. Then she put some serious wiggle into her walk.

"Wow!" said Bubba. "Is she smoking or what?"

"Wow is right. She's something else."

Fifteen minutes went by and still no sign of our waitress. I was getting edgy about our gear being unattended so long. But that didn't shake me up as much as when the two cops from our near arrest walked into the café from a side door and sat down only a couple of booths over from us. A pile of newspapers was heaped on the table next to us, so I reached over and snatched a couple sections; we then fanned them out to conceal our identities.

"Where's our waitress," I snapped. The cops were no more situated in their booth when I heard the whistle of a southbound waling in the distance. A couple minutes later the windows rattled and the foundation of the small building shook when four

Southern Pacific southbound engines rumbled past outside.

"If our food doesn't come soon might miss the chance to catch out on the southbound that just rolled past," I whispered.

"How do we get past those cops?"

"I'm working on it."

Finally we spotted our pretty waitress prancing over toward our table, clutching a grease stained bag in one hand, and sodas in the other.

"I paid the bill and gave her a buck extra, while explaining our strange predicament. And that we somehow needed to get past the two cops in the booth a couple tables over, because we needed to be on the southbound freight that had just rolled into town.

"Don't you worry about a thing sugar," she giggled deviously. "I'll take care of the boys in blue, while you and the stud make your grand get away."

If anyone could pull it off, it was her. Then she pranced over to their booth and did what she did best. They seemed to know her. When she bent over the table to reach for a bottle of ketchup very slow like, the copscop's eyes were super glued to her chest.

"That's our cue," I whispered."

We tiptoed right past them, and out the door we went. I stuffed the food and sodas into my pack on the run, as we bound toward the train. I couldn't believe my eyes; our train was already on the move. I sprinted alongside the closest car to me, a coal hopper and latched on to the ladder. Once my feet were secure in the foot rung, I positioned myself to give Bubba a hand up.

"Come on kid you can do it!" I shouted over the screeching wheels. He was running alongside the car, out stretching his hands. He grimaced and lunged forward. When I felt the warmth of his hand in mine, I clamped down like a vice. As his feet left the ground, my arm felt as though it was being jerked clean out the socket. On his swing toward the car his feet missed the foot rung altogether and dangled between deadly wheels. I gritted my teeth and pulled back with all my might. On his swing back, he was able to secure them. Then I scaled the ladder, tossed my pack over the edge, and climbed back down, and grabbed Bubba's gear. Then we scaled the ladder. We straddled the top lip of the car and watched until the lights of Klamath Falls faded away on the horizon. Afterwards, I flung Curtis's pack over the side. Then we slid down the steep incline. At the bottom, we were forced to lie on our sides, inside the narrow trap doors, where the coal was dispersed from, making very uncomfortable accommodations for us.

"Let's eat," Bubba said.

I finagled my pack around to get at the food. Our burgers were smashed, and the fries crushed. But at least the sodas survived the incident. The steep angle of the coal chuteshoot made ittough to sit up, forcing us to eat our on our sides.

"Wow! Check out the stars," Bubba said, with his mouth full.

They were so thick and brilliant, and with such clarity I was literally blown away. They looked like cut diamonds against the black velvet sky. It looked as though we could almost reach out and touch them. Even the Milky Way was three dimensional against the backdrop of space. Bubba began to spout out the names of many well-known constellations, and a few I'd never heard of. I was amazed by his knowledge of the universe.

"How is it that you know so much about astronomy?" I asked with astonishment.

"I've been into the stars since I can remember. On clear nights at my dad's house, back home in Texas, I climb out onto the roof next to my bedroom window with my telescope. Sometimes I stay out there for hours gazing at the stars and moon. I've read pert near every science fiction book, I could get my hands on, since I could read," he said boastfully.

"I figured you for a reader. You've already read every book in my pack and are now reading some for the second time."

"I guess I have," he grinned.

I've always been infatuated with the stars myself, but never took the time to study 'em as you have. But I've a lot of science fiction books throughout the years. Especially any book involving space travel, those are my favorite. Space travel has always infatuated me."

"Me too!" Bubba blurted out. "Wouldn't it be bitchin' if me and you had our own spaceship and we traveled the galaxy together?"

"That would be way beyond cool."

Then he started spouting out some of the titles of science fiction books he had read through the years. I had also some of the same the same books.

We lay there and scanned the vast universe before us, in hope of spotting some shooting stars, satellites, or even U.F.O.'s.

"Bring on the light show." Bubba shouted, when a huge shooting star streaked across the universe, with a long tail of stardust blazing behind it.

In the next couple of hours we saw at least a dozen shooting stars, and managed to pick out several satellites. Unfortunately, we weren't able to spot any U.F.O's.

Later I told Bubba to check out another shooting star. But he didn't respond. I looked over and saw that he was fast asleep. Under the starlight he looked though he was smiling and at peace.

I reached over and ruffled his curly locks. "Sleep well my little brother.

As I lay there gazing into the vast heavens above, I felt in total sync with the universe and suspected God's hand was involved in this very rare occurrence. Not in my entire life had I seen the stars in such multitude, or so brilliant in the night sky.

"All things on the earth are alive," I could hear my Native American, friend, Lonesome Walt's voice, echoing in my thoughts.

"Lonesome Walt's belief is that everything is a living being, including the stars, mountains, trees, hills, rivers and streams.

I had the honor of riding the rails and living on the land with Lonesome Walt and his son, Little Lonesome, for about a month a couple years ago. In that time, Lonesome and his son had taught me how to embrace the true meaning of life, and live in peace and harmony. Most importantly, they taught me how to have a greater respect and admiration towards Mother Earth. By the time we parted roads, I had a much deeper understanding of the universe.

I wondered if the Native Americans, before the white man came, experienced these rare occurrences more frequently, while living free and in harmony on the open land.

Eventually the steady drone of the rumbling wheels beneath pulled me down into peaceful dreams of living on the land in harmony with Lonesome Walt, Little Lonesome, and their people long ago: Clickety Clack! Clickety Clack! Clickety Clack!

CHAPTER 12

When I woke my body felt as though it had molded to the shape of the coal chute. When I went to move, my body did not respond. My first thought was panic. But with each small effort, I was able to move a little more, until finally I was able to sit up. The train was stopped but I had no way of knowing of our whereabouts. I did know however, I wasn't staying in the bottom of that coal hopper a minute longer, even if it meant catching another train. I nudged Bubba and told him get up. It was a must we get out of that car.

"I think I'm paralyzed," he groaned, as he tried to lift his head. It even took him a bit of work before he was able to sit up.

We were both so stiff and sore from lying in the bottom of the trap doors; we had a tough time trying to climb the steep grade up the side of the car. Once at the top, we sat on the lip of the car until we caught our breath. Then we hobbled down the ladder like two rickety old men. Even from the ground, I wasn't able to see the front or the rear of the train. I assumed we had been switched off while sleeping. But I did, however, recognize our location. We were in a small yard on the outskirts of Mount Shasta, California.

Ambling down the service road beneath the shadow of the fourteen thousand foot Mount Shasta that loomed over us like a sleeping giant, the uncanny feeling that we were being watched crept uponinto me. There was such a cathedral hush in the air that not a whisper of wind, a sound of a cricket, frog, or any other critter could be heard, only our breathing and the gravel shuffling beneath our feet. I scorned Bubba more than once for dragging his boots in the stones. As we rounded a bend on the track, we spotted the caboose down the line about twenty cars from us.

"At least we know we haven't been switched off," I said. "Now if we can find something to ride, we'll be styling."

It was a good sign when the lights were on inside the caboose, when we walked behind it. From there we walked back toward the front of the train. The third car up, was an open Southern Pacific boxcar, only open on that side. I scanned the interior with my flashlight, then we swung up inside. Bubba was about to roll out when I stopped him.

"I'm tired," he snapped.

"In less than an hour this train will pull into Dunsmuir to change crews. Say we jump off and take a break from for a day or two? I don't know about you, but I'm ready for a rest. There's a stream near the jungle known for its excellent trout fishing. And town is in walking distance. Dunsmuir isn't Wishram, but it's still an awesome place to kickback."

Bubba hesitated, as though he were in thought. "Why not, I'm ready for a break myself."

"I forewarn you though; the dick in that yard has a reputation. He doesn't usually bother hobos much camped out in the jungle. But we can't let him catch us on his train. Rumor has it, he's been known to set tramps gear on fire, and knock em'em around some, with his night stick. He likes to sit in his vehicle at night and shine his spot light into and onto all the cars when the train rolls into the yard, or out of the yard.

"I ain't afraid of no railroad bull," Bubba boasted, sticking out his chest.

When the train pulled into Dunsmuir we laidied flat on our bellies, in the front of the car, until well after it came to a stop. Eventually, we worked up the courage to creep over to the door and peek out. Luckily, the open door was on the wooded side of the track, the same side as the camp. All looked clear, so we jumped down and scurried off into the trees and stayed under their cover until we arrived at the jungle. By then it was already getting light. We were so exhausted,; we immediately rolled out our bedrolls and crawled inside them. Soon the rhythmic melody of the gurgling stream behind us, saing me to sleep.

CHAPTER 13

When I woke, the sun was up in a cloudless sky and a warm southwestern sighed through the trees above. I sat up, stretched and yawned. It was another perfect spring afternoon. Taking a bath was the only thing on my mind. If memory served me correctly, there was a swimming hole not more than a couple of hundred yards upstream from the jungle that was plenty deep to bathe in. I jumped up and pulled out a clean change of clothes from my pack, soap, a washcloth and towel, then headed off for the stream.

The swimming hole was exactly where I remembered it. I shed my clothes. I let out a hellacious yelp when I plunged into the icy waters. I wasted no time soaping down and rinsing off. Then I jumped back out. However, afterwards, I felt exhilarated and happy to be clean once again.

The kid was still zonked when I got back to camp. Then I started a fire and got coffee on. Before long, the percolator gurgled and the rich smell of java swirled around the jungle. I pulled the pot off, still percolating, and poured myself a steaming cup.

Later I fished out my journal. Leafing through the notebook, I read past entries. Going over them brought back memories, some stirred emotions and others made me laugh. They were the closest thing to reliving some of the most extraordinary experiences that had occurred during my travels throughout America from the other side of the tracks. As I read, I realized how blessed I had been to have such freedom. Some people I knew back home thought I was a lowlife, no account bum, and plum crazy, because of this life I chose to live. *OIf only if they could taste this life so free*, I thought, *only then would their eyes be opened to see.*

It took me over an hour to update the journal, but Bubba was still sleeping. I wanted to go to town to pick up a few odds and ends, but didn't want to leave him alone,. yYet no one seemed to be around. In fact, it looked as though there hadn't been any activity in the camp for quite sometime. So, I took a chance and headed into town.

When I got back the kid was awake, but still in his bedroll. He yawned and stretched: "What's in the bag?"

"It's past two in the afternoon. Get up lazybones."

His eyes bugged out when I pulled out a dozen eggs, a pound of bacon, a loaf of bread, along with a few other goodies.

He sprung out from beneath his sleeping-bag like a jack rabbit. Let's eat," he said, smacking his lips.

"You go bathe in the stream, while I get breakfast started."

"I'm not dirty!" he protested.

"That's a matter of opinion. Your face is filthy and your hair is all matted together. You have what hobo's refer to as, freight-train hair."

"What's freight train hair?" he snarled.

"It's when you've been riding trains for a couple of days and your hair gets all tangled and matted from the wind, and funky from dirt that floats around the tracks. It's nasty. No wash, no eat, end of discussion!"

He shot me a dirty look: "Being with you is worse than being in prison!"

"My mom always says: 'Being poor, is no excuse to be dirty."

He rummaged through his bag and pulled out a change of clothes, then stomped off toward the creek mumbling under his breath.

A couple of minutes later I heard a shriek loud enough to wake the dead come from the creek. Everyone in town must have heard him. Later he walked back into camp all spiffed up, looking good and even better spirits.

"How many eggs, and how do ya like 'em?"

"Scrambled and as many as I can.

"Scrambled it is."

He beamed from ear to ear when I handed him a bowl heaped with six scrambled eggs, a half of pound of bacon, two slices of bread that I had toasted over the fire, and a steaming cup of coffee. We had no trouble wolfing down the succulent breakfast fitr for kings.

"What made you start ridin' trains?" Bubba asked with piece of bacon hanging out of his mouth.

"Hugo Mackie?"

"Who's Hugo Mackie?"

"He's a close friend ofs Dad's. Hugo is an engineer for the Chessie System Railroad. As I grew up, he shared many of his railroad adventures with me, from back in the late forties and early fifties, when he was a fireman for the Marquette Railroad. It was his job to shovel the coal into the belly of the old steam locomotive. Hugo is a true adventurer, a kindred spirit. He owns a thirty two foot wood, Chris Craft cabin cruiser, the "Debanshur." The boat is named after is wife, Ann, and his two daughters, Debbie and Shural. Arnie and I were always off on some crazy escapade with his dad on that damn boat, usually when Hugo was three sheets into wind. Lake Michigan is a big lake. I'm telling you this because, once he woke Arnie and me in the middle of the night, saying he needed a crew to help sail the Debanshur across Lake Michigan, to the Wisconsin side. That's about an eighty mile stretch of open water. It can get downright ugly out in the big lake in a heartbeat. Many ships have perished in Lake Michigan in bad weather through the years. Just the same, we felt honored to be a part of this grand scheme. We were about half way across, before Hugo sobered up enough to realize his insane gesture. It was daylight by then. Sop Hugo let Arnie and I swim off the back of the boat for a couple hours, in water so pure and clean, we were able to see the boat's entire bottom boat, under water more than fifty feet away without wearing goggles. Back aboard,Then he turned the Debanshur around and we headed for home.

On our homeward voyage, a heavy fog rolled in, and we almost rammed by a monstrous coal ship.

"Bitiful!' Bitiful!'Bitiful! Was all Hugo had to say about our near death encounter with the thousand foot ship? We waved at the crew standing on the deck, not more than fifty feet away as the good ship ambled on past.

Sometimes, Hugo would take us and his cronies out into Lake Michigan, on moon lit nights and drop the anchor just off the shore at a place they referred to as Kenny's camping spot."

"Where's Kenny's camping spot?"

"Kenny's camping spot is a stretch of an unoccupied beach, a couple miles north of the White Lake channel."

"Who's Kenny?"

"Kenny is one of Hugo's closest friends," I said irritably. "He's the person who founded the spot."

"After we dropped the hook, we'd wade into shore with a bunch of food and drink. Then we'd make a huge bonfire and have one hell of a cookout. Our after dinner entertainment usually consisted of Hugo's pal, Dick Palish playing the accordion, sometimes until dawn. Arnie and I were usually passed out on the beach by then. Those are just a couple of the misadventures I experienced with Hugo Mackie. I think, what makes him so interesting, is the fact that he is so spontaneous!? You never know what he's gonna do at any given moment. Most everything he does is on the spur of the moment."

"He sounds like a fun dad to have."

"He's the best."

Suddenly Bubba got quiet. I sensed he was thinking about home.

"Like I said earlier, this stream is known for good trout fishing. I've stayed here before, but never tried my luck. So what do you say we get out the gear and slay some trout?"

"You mean it!"

"Yeah I mean it, how do you think we're gonna eat the next couple of days."

I pulled out my telescoped fishing rod, and Mitchell open bale reel from my pack. I have some wet flies we can try. Let's see what kind of damage we can do."

"Trout fishing is a little trickier than lake fishing," I explained, while rigging the four pound test monofilament line, with a slip bobber, and a small split shot, just enough weight for casting. Whenever fishing for trout, always walk down stream, because they face into the current to feed on debris that floats down to them. Also remember, they can feel vibration in the water when someone walks along the bank. So walk gently, as not to spook em'em."

"Can I have the pole now?," he pleaded.

"Are you even listening," I snapped. "Just hold on to your shorts a minute. I want to show you a thing or two before you get started,. t Then I'll hand it over. Whenever you spot a trout in the water, always cast up stream, far enough above the fish, so the bait naturally floats down to it.

I made a few casts to give him the idea of the rhythm and technique of stream fishing, and then handed him the rig.

"She's all yours, now catch us some lunch."

He let out a war whoop when he tied into his first fish, a few minutes later. The trout wasn't more than eight inches long, but neither of us had a fishing license anyway.

Later Bubba latched onto a good sized fish that put up a hell of a fight. The drag even sang out for a couple of minutes. I told him to keep his pole tip up and not to underestimate the trout's intelligence. Suddenly it made run for a log, wrapped the line around it, and was free to live another day. The kid stood in total disbelief, staring at the limp line as though, the fish were going to magically reappear back on. Unfortunately, the entire rig was gone, even the slip bobber.

"I've got more flies and bobbers; but it'll take a few minutes."

We sat on the bank while I started the re-rigging process.

"This reminds me of the time I had been picking rocks up in Madres, Oregon."

"What's picking rocks?"

"Up in that part of the country, after the farmer plows the field in the spring, its most usually peppered with rocks, tilled up from below the ground. The only way to remove them is to hire people to pick them up by hand. It's a dirty, back breaking job. No one really wants to do it, so they employ hobos and immigrants.

"How do they get the rocks out of the field?

"The farmer pulls what is called a stone boat, behind a tractor, alongside the workers. The workers pretty stay bent over all day, and throw rocks into the wagon as fast they can. The first day is living hell, let me tell ya. By the end of it, a person can barely stand up straight. The work would usually last only a few days. By then you're ready for it to be over anyway.

"What does that have to do with fishing?"

"If you hold on, I'll tell ya. After the rock picking was finished, I caught the local Union Pacific train out of Madres, on my way up to Wishram to hang out for a few days."

"The Wishram we didn't get to go you mean?"

"Yeah, that's the one and only."

"North of Madras, the train pulled into a siding alongside a river that paralleled the tracks. So I jumped up to see what was going on. An older man and a younger guy climbed down out of the caboose with fishing rods in their hands and walked down to the stream. Their lines hypnotically arched over again and a gain and settled upon the water's surface like glinting threads of silver. When suddenly, bang, the younger man's line taauuntened, and his pole doubled over asnd the drag sang out like the fat lady at the opera."

"Keep that pole tip up," the old timer shouted, his voice hoarse with excitement.

I was so consumed by the action that I actually fell out of the boxcar, and skinned up my knees. The man would gain a few feet until the fish retaliated and took back ten more feet. This battle went on and on, making it tough for the brakeman to gain any serious headway toward the bank. Then the silver monster torpedoed out of the water and did a fantailed dance on the surface, trying every trick it knew to shake that hook. Again and again, I watched it dance upon the surface, its silver jeweled glory glittering under the afternoon sun like rhinestones stones."

"Be careful!," shouted the old timer, "he's a crafty som bitch."

Then the great trout dove toward deeper water and the drag began to sing again. Then it was as though the trout of trout's accepted defeat and swam toward the bank. The brakeman reeled his line in as fast as he could, while the old timer got the net ready to scoop their prize. The granddaddy of trout's, however, had something else in mind. When it cruised past their feet, and then the net, it did a quick about face and took off lighting fast for deeper water. The line made a loud crack when it snapped. There must have been slack in it for all I could figure. The old timer stood on the bank with the same dumbfounded look you just had, as though his prize were going to magically reappear back onto the line. If that wasn't bad enough, the crafty old devil torpedoed out of the water one last time to let them know just what they missed out on. I thought the old guy was gonna break down and cry on the spot. They then walked back to the caboose, heads bowed, with the agony of defeat written upon their faces. I suspected the old guy had been trying to catch that fish for quite some time."

"Hand me a fly," I said "then you'll be ready to tear em'em up."

After I tied on the fly, I handed him back the pole back.

"Now get out there and catch our dinner."

I didn't care about the fishing as much as I enjoyed watching the kid having the time of his life.

That evening we came returned to camp with a mess of nice trout, fourteen in all, some better than twelve inches long.

Before I could make dinner we were going to need a few things. But I didn't have time to run to the store. It was going to be dark in a couple of hours. So I asked Bubba if he'd mind picking up some flour, eggs, and a couple of other odds and ends. He was thrilled I was going to let him go alone. I reached into my wallet and pulled the last of our money. We were now officially broke. From that point on, we were going to have to rely upon God's good graces. I didn't say anything to the kid. Why spoil a perfectly good day. He'd find out soon enough.

"Pick up a candy bar to treat yourself for a job well done.

"You mean it?"

"Yeah I mean it; you did a hell of a job today kid. I'm proud of ya.

Because of you, we're gonna eat like royalty tonight. In fact, you did such a good job; I'm even going to let you help me clean the fish when you get back."

"Wow," he said sarcastically, before taking off for town.

I started the filleting process, with my fishing, fillet knife, while he was ran his errand.

When Bubba got back to camp he had a worried look was on his face.

"What's wrong?" I asked.

"When I was in the store, a big man walked inside and told me that he was the Railroad Detective and that he knew we were camped out, down here in the jungle. He also told me to tell you, he'd be waiting for us when we tried to get back on his train."

"Don't you worry about him? He'll have to catch us first. The way I see it, he'll be expecting us to jump on near the jungle. But we won't be anywhere near here, thanks to him. Neither will we get into a boxcar. Instead, we'll catch out on a car carrier, if there is one. A risky move, but I don't think he'll be expecting it. We'll deal with him when the time comes. The moment he threatened us, it became a challenge."

A broad smile broke across his face. "It'll be like in the movies."

"You got it kid."

Bubba helped me clean the rest of the fish. After we finished up, we had a good couple pounds of pure unadulterated trout meat heaped in a bowl. Afterwards, we walked over to the stream and dumped the fish remains into the water and then washed up to get the fish smell off us.

Back at camp, I broke three eggs into a clean bowl and whipped them into a liquid with my fork. Bubba dipped the fillets into egg yoke and then rolled them in the flour, while I dropped them in to the hot bacon grease, left over from breakfast, as fast as he rolled them. The succulent fillets crackled and grease splattered as they dropped into the hot liquid. Bubba and I were popping the pan fried filets into our mouths as fast as they came out of the pan. They melted in our mouths like butter on a hot muffin, and tasted like a piece of heaven. Before we were through frying them up, we were both so stuffed,; neither of us could finish the rest. Our dessert consisted of coffee and a pack of Twinkies, we split between us.

Later that evening we pulled our bedrolls out away from beneath the tree, so we could star gaze. As we lay beneath the diamond studded black velvet sky, both with full bellies, we talked about girls, fast cars and space travel. Later a southbound freight rolled into the yard. Every time the detective made a pass he'd shine his spotlight toward the camp. After the train departed, we lay there and watched the night sky, until the soothing rhythm of the laughing brook swept us away.

For the next couple days we fished the stream during the day and star gazed at night and talked about girls, fast cars and space travel.

CHAPTER 14

On the third night, old dirty face called down from top the mountain top like an old friend.

Bubba and I sprung up at the same time, looked at each other, and laughed, both of us on the same page. So we jumped up and started packing.

The railroad detective was already on the prowl. When ever he made a pass, he'd direct his spotlight toward the jungle. Once packed, we scurried off into the woods and stayed beneath the cover of the trees, working our way further down the tracks.

"So far so good," I gasped. "This guy takes his job pretty serious."

"This is like being in a movie," Bubba snickered, "and we're trying to escape from a Nazi concentration camp."

We dove for the ground when five Southern Pacific engines rumbled past. Then we crawled on our hands and knees over as close to the tracks as we dared to look for a car carrier. More than once we had to dive onto our stomachs to avoid the roving eye of the detective's spotlight. My heart skipped a beat when two open boxcars rolled past. But I knew we had to hold out. Then I saw what we were looking for, the silhouettes of two car carriers rolling our way. After the train stopped the carriers were still a couple of hundred feet back down the track from us. We waited for the dick to make another pass, then, we jumped and ran for the carriers.

"Go to the second car back," I said. "The top tier looks like new pickup trucks. We're in luck,; it's one of the older models, with no roof over the top. We had no more scaled the ladder up to the third tier, when the roving one eyed monster came our way again. We tossed the packs over into the bed a pickup. Then we dove flat on our stomachs, onto the deck. The bull's bronco slammed on the brakes. Then his light slowly scanned over and over the two car carriers. My heart pounded so hard, my fingertips felt as though they were going to explode. I thought for sure we were busted until he was on the prowl again. Hurriedly, we jumped up and dove into the back of the truck and laid low. After what seemed like eternity, the train finally rolled forward. The detective sat in his vehicle and swept every car with his spotlight as the train rolled slowly out of the yard. When his spotlight made a sweep over the top of the pickup, neither of us moved a muscle, until we were well out of Dunsmuir. Then we rolled out our bedrolls under the canopy of stars draped over us and fell asleep to the sweet symphony of the, Clickety Clack, Clickety Clack, Clickety Clack!

CHAPTER 15

The high pitch squeal of brakes startled me awake. I sat up and looked out over the side of the pickup bed. The sun had begun to peak over the surrounding mountains tops. Above I could also see the long train wrapped around the switchbacks on side of the mountain like a long twisting snake. Sections of the train were shrouded in clouds, giving the delusion that there was more than one train up there. I woke Bubba and told him to him to check it out.

"Look!" He said pointing. "There's more than one train there."

"It's all the same train; it looks that way because of the way the clouds are shrouded around the side of the mountain, also because the way the long train is wrapped around the switchbacks."

"Bitchin!"

The smell of fresh vegetation and earth rose to greet us as the train descended from the southern slope, and the land spread open before us.

As we rolled out onto the flatland, the engineer opened the throttle and we were making good time once again. Later we passed enormous crop farms stretching out as far as the eye could see. For no apparent reason, Bubba jumped up and stretched out his arms and said: "I'm flying, I'm flying," repeatedly.

I yelled at him to sit down; terrified he'd be ejected from the bed of the truck and cast down to a horrid death. But he utterly refused unless I agreed to at least give it a try. Knowing his stubbornness, I stood up only to appease him. At first I was a little oozy, until stabilized. I had to admit, the view was incredible. I could see the full length of the train, front to rear that was at least at least a mile long. Our car was closer to the rear. To the west, I could also see the coastal mountains silhouetted against a cloudless blue canvas. To stand so high above the open land gave me the exhilarating feeling of flying. A chill shot down my spine, remembering once again why I loved the freedom of the road.

"Yee haw!" I shouted, "We're free! We're free!"

"Yee haw," yelled Bubba. "I'm going home and I'm free!"

Suddenly, the car jerked when rolling over a stretch of rough track, knocking us off our feet, and flat onto our asses. We rolled around in the pickup bed laughing hysterically, but agreed it might be a good idea to push our luck again.

We watched the town Chico zing past us like a blur.

"If we keep this up," I said, "we should roll into Roseville early this afternoon. "

"Do ya think we'll catch another train out, yet today," Bubba asked excitedly.

"I hate to break it to ya kid, we are now officially flat broke. It's a must I pick up some kind spot labor that pays daily. Two days pay should get us the rest of the way to Dallas."

"Shit! Not another damn delay."

"Keep your chin up, I'll get ya home. But it's no picnic to be destitute."

The higher the sun climbed into to the afternoon sky, the hotter it got in the pickup bed. After Biggs,

I pulled my journal from my pack to make an entry. At the time Bubba was propped against the back window reading.

I find the freedom of the road, truly a gift. What I cherish most about it, is how unpredictable it can be, and how abruptly life can change course. You never know what adventures are lurking around the next bend, or what to expect from one minute to the next. Everyday on the road is a wonder and a challenge in it self. However, when life does make an abrupt turn for the worst, you learn to hang on tight and ride out the storm.

Although Curtis and I have suffered some hardships since our departure from Yakima, I'm awed by his resilience to adapt to the challenges we have had to face. It also does my heart good to see that he views the world around him with such wonder and excitement. Beyond the shadow of doubt, Curtis is a kindred spirit. With each passing day, he becomes more the little brother I never had, and less the pain in the backside he was in the beginning this quest.

We now face a new challenge. We are flat broke. This predicament throws me into the position to be assertive and creative. However, going into an unknown town, where nobody knows anything about us, and then finding gainful employment, I've always felt insecure about, even though I've done it on countless occasions. If life on the road has taught me anything, is that one does not control their destiny; rather your destiny controls you. More and more, everyday I learn to let go of my petty worries and put my trust in God himself.

I set down the journal, yawned, stretched, and then gazed out across the open land zinging past. I noticed that the warm air swirling around me felt cooler than earlier, even semi- pleasant. Yet the sun was high in a cloudless sky. I estimated the temperature in the mid-70s. Bubba was zonked out on his sleeping bag. I stretched out, deciding to get some shut eye before the train rolled into Roseville. I lay there with many thoughts bouncing around inside my head. Eventually I drifted off to rhythm of the, Clickety Clack Clickety Clack.

I barely closed my eyes, when I felt someone tugging on my arm.

"I think we're coming into the Roseville," Bubba yelled.

I sat up and looked around. Sure enough the train was making the final approach into the yard.

"The train will most likely roll in front of the yard tower. So we'd be pushing our luck to enter the yard in the back of a brand new pickup if ya know what I'm saying.

While scaling down the ladder to the bottom tier, the car rocked violently back and forth, while rolling over joining tracks, making the experience more than a little scary. Then we crawled over to the other side of the car that would be hidden from the tower, and lay low on our stomachache until it slowed enough for us to bail off on the fly. We then ducked into a row of nearby railcars after we bailed. From there we threaded through a maze of railcars until we found a service road.

"Stay close to me," I said. This yard is the main hub for the Southern Pacific Railroad and its huge and easy to get lost in.

We were just about out of the yard when we came upon four older guys in a jungle, sitting around a camp fire, downing some cold brews.

"Do you guys know of any day labor going on around here," I asked.

"Heard about some work up around Marysville, a few days back," said a tall lanky man. "I'm Mountain Dew.

"I'm Lord Open road," said another.

"I'm Hobo herb," said another, "and this is Slow Motion Shorty."

"I'm Free Bird and this is Bubba Lee, out of Texas.

"It's good to meet ya," Bubba and said at the same time.

"If ya boys are hungry, we got sandwiches coming out of our ears. Shorty retrieved them out of a dumpster, behind a vending machine outfit."

"Yeah, we haven't eaten since we caught out of Dunsmuir."

"You were up in Dunsmuir?" said Mountain Due. "Heard that yard was hot. I guess there was some trouble in the jungle a couple weeks back."

"I wondered why it was so desolate around there.

"That bull can be plain ornery," said Slow Motion Shorty, "when he gets a bug up his ass." You're lucky he didn't catch you on his train.

"I thought we were busted for sure when we were on top of the car carrier we rode in on," I said. "I was sweating bullets when his spotlight scanned over and over the car. We camped out there for a couple days, but he never bothered us."

"You're lucky," said Hobo Herb. "Somebody is gonna kill 'iem someday."

"You boys go ahead and eat all the sandwiches you want," said Mountain Dew.

We took him up on his generous invitation and stuffed ourselves until either of us could eat another bite. Afterwards, Mountain Dew gave us each two more for the road.

"Thanks for the grub, and the tip on the spot labor," I said. We're gonna make our way on up to Marysville, I Guess. With some luck, we might score some work tomorrow."

"Take care boys, you hear," all four men said at the same time.

"Those guys were old school hobos like Buzz," I said. "Did you notice how neat they're camp was? They were the genuine article, my friend, true hobos, gallant nights of the open road."

While crossing over a bridge that spanned across a small creek, I remembered that there was a swimming hole beneath it. Tramps that knew about the hole, used it for bathing, and swam there to beat the heat. So I turned around headed back for the creek.

"Now what are you doing?" said Bubba, with attitude.

"There's a swimming hole beneath this bridge. I'm gonna go clean up.   Keep an eye out, I don't need to be cited for indecent exposure."

I assumed he'd have a tizzy fit if I suggested he clean up again.   But that wasn't stopping me though. I grabbed a bar of soap, towel and a change of clothes from my pack. Then I walked beneath the bridge along the waters edge until I reached the water hole. Afterwards, I shed my clothes and then plunged in. The water was almost bath warm. After soaping up, I dove back in and rinsed off.

"Hurry up" Bubba's voice echoed beneath the bridge, "I'm next."

The water was so warm; I had tough time getting out.

Afterwards, Bubba took his turn. But he refused to get out of the water until I threatened to leave him there.

We managed to pan handle enough money in down town Roseville, to take city transportation to the edge of town. From there we hoofed over to State Road 65, and then started hitching it.   A couple of minutes later an old beat up Chevy pickup pulled over onto the shoulder. I walked up to the driver side window and asked how far they were going. The driver was a Hispanic man. His man English was broken, but I understood Marysville clearly. The women sitting close to him, I assumed was his wife. They both looked to be in their forties. He motioned for us to jump in the back. We tossed our gear in the bed of the pick-up then hopped in. I was ecstatic we caught a ride so soon and hoped that that was a sign of good fortune to come. We sat with our backs against the rear window enjoying the cool air swirling around us. Bubba didn't say much though. I suspected he was still pissed at me about our detour. I didn't blame him, but I wasn't about to cross the barren desert with no food or money. Besides, we still had a long way before we reached Dallas. *It's my job to take care of him,* I thought to myself.

When the driver dropped us off in downtown Marysville, Bubba walked up to his window and spoke fluent Spanish to him and the lady. As they drove off, the man stuck his arm out the window and waved.

"I didn't have a clue that you spoke Spanish," I said, in astonishment.

"Spanish is like a second language in Texas."

"Kid you're full of surprises."

From there we set out to look for the railroad tracks, in hope of finding a place to jungle out for the night. Along the way, we made a stop at a Laundromat and ate a sandwich inside, while taking the liberty of free air-conditioning.

"We're gonna have to get up before dawn and hoof it over to a temp service," I said, with my mouth full. "If lady luck is with us, I should score a day or two of work. Then we'll be back out on the road again."

"That's what I'm talking about!" Bubba said, as he high fived me.

The camp I had in mind was already occupied. There were two men standing over a small fire. As we neared the jungle, I thought I recognized both of them. Just then a dog walked out toward us, growling, and snarling and showing its teeth, sniffing the air. Then it started wagging its tail.

"Mr. Murphy, you old scoundrel," I said, as I stooped down to scratch him behind the ears.

"You and me was about to lock horns young ones," said the Native American man staggering toward us.

"How's it goin' Lonesome?"

He stopped, stared at me queerly for a moment, until he recognized me.

"Why if it ain't Free Bird," he said in his sing soang voice. "Come, sit with us and have a drink. Who's the young buck?"

"This is Bubba Lee, out of Texas," I said laughing. Bubba meet Lonesome Walt."

By then, Lonesome's son, Little Lonesome had walked over to greet us.

"Bubba, this is Lonesome Walt, and his son Little Lonesome. Last but not least, this is Mister Murphy."

If there was anyone in the world I wanted more at the moment, it was them. They were both my mentors. Pretty much everything I had learned about riding trains, which important anyway, was from them. I even had the honor of making

147

their acquaintance a couple summers before, back in Wihshram, Washington and ended up hanging out with them for well over a month. Before then, I had never carried pots and pans or cooking utensils on my person. I had pretty much had eaten only, whenever, or wherever I had a chance. These guys had even taught me how to retrieve perfectly good food from dumpsters, behind grocery stores. And then prepare gourmet meals with the food, on the smallest of fires. (Lonesome had told me countless times, only the white man makes big fires.) I spent many summer evenings, listening to Lonesome speak of the ways of his people while sitting around the campfire, and of the way they had once lived so free on the open land. From time to time Lonesome would chant in his Native tongue and demonstrate ceremonial dances his people had performed for different rituals in the past. Although Lonesome was in his mid sixty's, his light brown complexion, and his facial skin was so smooth, he looked youthful. He stood around five, six, with an average build. His cheekbones were high and his nose was squatted. He had a round cheerful face, and grayish black hair. Lonesome was very much into his Native heritage. He often spoke of his ancestors. And how his people lived in peace before the white man came and robbed them of their land and their free way of life. Although he drank quite heavily, Walt had never shown any sign of anger or violence toward me.

Unlike his father, Little Lonesome stood over six feet. He had broad shoulders and jet black hair down to the middle of his back that was usually braded. His facial features were similar to his fathers, but his nose was a bit larger and more squatted. Little Lonesome was quite a handsome young man to say the least.

He was seventeen when we met back in Wishram. Little Lonesome was very traditional in the ways of his people and was deeply involved in tribal affairs. He often spoke of the Creator, and how much respect he had for every thing existing upon Mother Earth. Little Lonesome didn't believe in getting drunk either. He'd only take the occasional swig out of respect for his father. He also always carried a medicine bag on his person. Though, he never spoke of it, I sensed he was a spiritual person among his people, possibly a shaman. Whenever I was in Little Lonesome's presence, the words peace, harmony and profound came to mind.

Mr. Murphy was no ordinary dog either. Walt told me, in the past, Murphy was half pit-bull and half dingo. His coat was reddish brown with stripes. He had the most intelligent eyes, I've ever seen in a dog. Whenever he looked me, I got the eerie feeling he was reading my thoughts.

"Sit down and have a drink," slurred Lonesome, as he handed me a bottle of White port wine.

"Don't mind if we do," I said.

"How are ya doing," Lonesome," I asked.

"You know, been runnin' up and down the tracks, between Minneapolis and California. What brings ya to Marysville young one?"

"We're broke and down and out. I'm Hopin' I'll find some work here tomorrow."

"The Creator will guide you my brother," Little Lonesome chimed in.

"I know your right. He always has."

"Still toting all those books around?" I said to Little Lonesome.   "Aren't you supposed to be in school now?"

"Some of these are school books. I'm in college now. We're on spring break. Just came to hang out with pops for a few days."

"I've got a few books myself. Maybe we can do some swapping later on.   You like Louis L'Amour?"

"Interested in taking a peak at 'em."

I took another slug and then passed it to Little Lonesome. He took a small swig and passed the bottle to Bubba. Bubba looked at me for approval. I nodded. I'd allow a couple swigs so he'd feel like one of the gang.

"Bye the way, where's Slim Jim," I asked.

"Slim caught the westbound about a year ago," Walt said, bowing his head. His liver gave out on him.   Why me and Slim tramped the country together for more than twenty years."

"Sorry to hear that. I always liked Slim. I suspected you had been together for a while."

When the bottle came back, I lifted it, and proposed a toast that Slim's spirit live out on the rail to the end of time."

"I'll drink to that we all agreed. Afterwards, we each took a slug.

Bubba and Little Lonesome hit it off almost instantaneously. In only a few minutes, Little Lonesome had all of his reading books spread out on the ground for the kid to rummage through them. So I pulled out all my books and handed them to Bubba."

"Now do some wheeling and dealing."

While they did their thing, I chatted with Walt. He caught me up on all the latest railroad gossip, mostly information about what switchyards were hot and what trains not to ride. When it came to the rail, Walt was a walking encyclopedia. He had more info stored away in his memory than I ever could hope to learn.

He also told me that he was pretty much broke as well. In fact, he had just spent his last couple of bucks on the bottle of wine we were sharing.

Since none of us had any money, Little Lonesome, Bubba and I decided to make a dumpster run behind a nearby supermarket.

"Bubba I want you to climb inside the dumpster with me," Little Lonesome said, while on our way to the supermarket. "It'll be easier for him to get in and out. I hope were not too early. The store should be tossing out their outdated produce and meat anytime now."

At the store I gave Little Lonesome and the kid a lift into the container.

"Our timing was perfect," Little Lonesome said, "the meat and produce are still cold."

It was my job to keep a look out for the cops and store employees while they pilfered through the goods. It was also my responsibility to stuff the food into a nylon bag, Little Lonesome used for such occasions. Our booty consisted of two large packages of out dated chuck steak, only by a day. They also found two pounds of out dated bacon, and various fruits and vegetables.

Little Lonesome and Bubba started preparations for supper as soon as we got back to camp. Within a half hour they had a batch of stew, with huge chunks of beef simmering in the gun boat. The entire time simmering; Bubba rubbed his belly and smacked his lips, saying over and over how hungry he was. Finally, little Lonesome ladled out some broth, veggies, and a couple chunks of meat into a bowl for him to snack on; I think to shut him up.

After consuming our delicious gourmet dinner fit for kings, we sat around the campfire and shot the breeze.

I said: Walt "Remember the time you, Slim, Little Lonesome, and Art the fart caught the California train out of Wishram? We were somewhere in Southern Oregon, when Art staggered over to the door to take a leak and accidentally stepped on Murphy. Then he kicked Murphy and told him to stay the hell out of his way. Murphy snarled at him and then glared at him for a few seconds. For the next day and half, whenever the train pulled into a siding, when you'd let Murphy down out of the car to take care of business, he wouldn't go. Then you got worried something was wrong with him. In the middle of the second night, I woke in time to watch Murphy trot over to where Art was passed out and lift his leg for what seemed like forever. Then he took a dump on him as well, and then he strutted back over to where you were, curled up and went back to sleep. The next day when Art finally came out of his alcohol induced coma, he realized he was drenched in dog piss, and shit on to boot, compliments of good old Mr. Murphy. For some strange reason Art never seemed to mess with Murphy after that.

Later Lonesome spoke of the history of his people, handed down to him by his forefathers, from generation to generation. He also spoke of how his people, at one time, before the white man came, had lived on the land in harmony. Then he performed some of the sacred dances of old around the campfire, while chanting in his native tongue. Bubba's eyes were glued to his every move. As the Walt's tales unfolded, I envisioned Bubba and me living on the land with him and Little Lonesome, along with their people, whose only purpose in life was to survive and never take more than what was necessary from Mother Earth. Eventually I slipped into vivid dreams of Bubba and me hunting, fishing and living in harmony on the land with Lonesome, Little Lonesome and their people.

CHAPTER 16

A westbound freight rumbling past out on the mainline startled me awake. I sprung up.

Everybody in camp was still asleep and the fire had dwindled down to coals. I wasn't sure what time it was, but birds were already chirping in the trees. So I jumped up and threw on some clothes and then started hoofing it toward the day labor place, Walt had told me about the night before. Along the way, I stopped at an all-night convenient mart to get a cup of coffee until I realized I was broke.

Several men were already milling around out in front of the labor office when I walked up. I asked someone if there had been much work out of there lately. He said work had been slow for quite some time. A few minutes later a pickup pulled up and a man rolled down the driver side window, asking for four men to do some concrete labor work. Because of my height and size, I was confident he'd pick me. But he took four guys who had worked for him before.

Ten o'clock came around and only two more jobs had gone out of there since. The situation looked bleak to say the least. I debated if I should even wait it out. My gut feeling told me that sticking around would be futile. So I took off to look for the nearest payphone. When I found one, I opened the phone book up to the yellow pages, under restaurants and searched for the addresses near the downtown area. Then I wrote down the addresses on a piece of paper. This technique had worked for me in the past. In fact, there was a certain restaurant in Salt Lake where they knew me well. And whenever I was in town, they'd always put me to work that same day pearl diving.

Although the pay wasn't the greatest, it was always cash under the table and a hot meal to boot.

I found the nearest restaurant and then walked inside and asked to speak to the manager. A couple of minutes later, a man who looked to be in his forties walked out and asked what he could do for me.

"Are you by chance in need of a dishwasher?" I asked.

"Yea, I need of a dishwasher," he said, "but it'll be two weeks before you get your first check."

"Is there any way I could get a draw?" I asked.

"Sorry, that's not the way we do things here."

"Ok thanks and have good day sir," I said, then took off.

Another restaurant needed dishwasher, but it was the same story. I was gonna try one more and then throw in the towel. At the last one, I spoke to a young woman, in her early thirties. Her name was Maggie. She said she was in desperate need of a dishwasher, because theirs had walked off the job day before.

"Can you start immediately?" she almost pleaded.

"Only if there's a way I can get an early advance the first day. After that I can hold off until I get my first paycheck. Otherwise no deal."

She thought for a moment. "If you finish out the day, I'll give you twenty bucks. Would that be enough to hold you over?"

"Barely, but we have a deal. Show me the way to the kitchen."

She shook my hand and then led the way. In the kitchen, she introduced me to the cook, and some of the waitresses who were taking turns trying to keep up with the dishes piled in stacks. She then handed me an apron. Lunch rush hour had already begun to get cranked up, so I jumped in up to my elbows and got started.

Once familiar with the machinery, I fell into a groove and was finally on top of things by 4 o'clock. Afterwards, I wiped everything down. The cook gave me smile of approval. Then he made me a half pound cheese burger and fries. I consumed the burger and fries, and then finished cleaning up. Around five o'clock, I walked up front. Maggie was more than happy with the job I'd done for her, and looked forward to seeing me at 6 am. Then she handed me twenty five bucks. It was hard to look her in the eye, knowing by 6:00 a.m., I planned to be back on the rail again.

"The extra five is my way of saying thanks for helping us out of a jam, she said with a warm smile.

On the way back to the jungle, I stopped at a store and picked up a bottle of White Port for Walt and couple things for Bubba and me, for the road.

Another important rule of the road was, if you had means, always return good for good. That way when you run into that person again, they'll be more apt to help you when down and out.

Mr. Murphy let out a ferocious roar as I approached jungle. Then he trotted out and bowed his head for me to scratch him behind the ears. Bubba was stretched out reading a novel that Little Lonesome had swapped with him the night before. Little Lonesome was frying up a batch of bacon that smelt so good, my mouth was salivating. Walt was sitting next to the fire looking sad and depressed because he was broke and out of booze. But his face lit up like Christmas tree when I pulled out the bottle of White Port wine and handed them to him.

Bubba jumped up and said, "How'd it go?"

"Not what I expected, but we have enough to get back on the road."

"Yee haw! You mean it! We can leave tonight?" he said with excitement.

"That's the plan. From here we'll catch the Western Pacific and ride her down into Stockton. From there we'll get back on the Southern Pacific and ride it down into to Colton, California."

"Where's Colton at?" Bubba asked excitedly.

"Colton is just east of Los Angeles."

"Yeah I'm going home!"

We sat around the fire and talked with Lonesome, and Little Lonesome, while Walt, happy as a lark, made love to his bottle of wine. At dusk a Western Pacific thundered past out on the mainline. Immediately I spotted an open boxcar.

"That's our baby if it stops, or slows down enough to catch out on it,' I said. Then the breaks screeched as the train slowed down. Bubba and I threw our gear together. Then we said our farewells to Lonesome and Little Lonesome.

Lonesome chanted in his Native tongue while Bubba and I said our farewells.

"My father asks that the Creator watch over you and Bubba the remainder of your journey." Little Lonesome translated.

"Thanks for being there for us in our time of need my friends," I said.

"Here we go again!" Bubba snickered as he flung his pack over his shoulder. Then we bound for the train. By then, it had had slowed plenty enough for us catch it on the fly.

"Run alongside the open boxcar," I shouted, "and then toss your pack inside the door and swing up the way I taught you."

He tossed his pack in, then swung up inside like a pro. I tossed him my bag and grabbed a hold of the latch and swung in. We stood in the doorway and waved at Lonesome, and Little Lonesome until their silhouettes disappeared into the evening dusk.

From out of the shadows, a tall distinguished looking man stepped up and startled us. He had well groomed short blond hair and his face was faire with freckles. He reminded me of an older version Robert Redford. Let's just say he wasn't your typical hobo.

"My name's Al," he said," with a genuine Robert Redford smile.

"I'm Freebird and this is Bubba Lee, out of Texas.

"Where are you boys off to?"

"Dallas, Texas," Bubba said boastfully.

"I'm on my way down to Indio, California."

"Does this train go to Stockton?" I asked.

"It breaks up there. Have you ever been in that yard?"

"Once."

"There's been a recent killing there. The yard is also a training facility for rookie railroad detectives. I heard the yard is super hot at the present. The word is, they're arresting anybody and everybody they catch in that yard, and giving dishing out ninety days in the clinker."

"Thanks for cheering us up," I said vexed. The last thing we need after what we've been through is trouble. If the train slows down enough, while rolling through Sacramento, the kid and I might bail off. From there it's easy to catch a bus over to Roseville.

"Suit your selves," Al said. "But I know my way around that yard well enough we shouldn't have a problem."

"Trains run south out of Stockton don't they?" I asked.

"Down to Bakersfield. Most trains break up in Bakersfield. Afterwards, they break the train down and rebuild it. Later part of it will continue south into Colton. But some trains some bypass Colton altogether, not many though."

Though Al seemed to know what he was talking about, my gut told me to go to Roseville.

"Aren't you a bit young to be riding freights," Al asked Bubba.

"I might be young," he said puffing out his chest, but I'm diggin' it all the same."

"That's good enough for me kid," Al chuckled.

The train rolled through Sacramento plenty slow enough for us to bail off. By then I had taken a liking to Al and decided to stick it out with him and take our chances.

Between Sacramento and Stockton, we were held up in a siding for more than a couple hours. When the train finally rolled into Stockton, it was a little after midnight.

"It's not the Western Pacific yard we need to worry about," Al said.

"There won't be any trains leaving the S.P. yard for a few hours, so we should try to get some sleep before we go tromping through the Southern Pacific yard. It'd be wise for us to be in the yard as little as possible. I know a safe place we can grab some shut eye between the two yards. Later we'll sneak over into S. P. yard and look for our train."

"Lead the way," I said in the middle of a yawn. Right now I'm so tired from working; I could sleep on a bed of nails.

Al led the way to a small patch of ground located in -between the two switchyards that was heavily over grown weeds that were about six feet tall, and down a narrow path that dead ended at the base of a small pond that was about a hundred feet in diameter. The pond, however, was mostly dried up except for only a couple of feet of muddy water at left the bottom. It looked as though it had been at least ten feet deep at one time. We rolled out our bedrolls on the dried, steep, cracked bank in an attempt to catch some zzz'ees.

A terrible nightmare about us being attacked by rats startled me awake. When I sat up, I was terrified. Part of my nightmare was true. There was a rat only feet from my face. Slowly I scanned the perimeter around the pond as not to spook them. I couldn't believe my eyes; the entire perimeter around the pond was covered with hundreds of rats. It looked as though they were creeping down to the bottom of the pond for a drink of water. I tried to whisper to Al, but I was so horrmortified, not a sound came out me. Finally, I worked up the courage to reach over and nudge him. Terror filled his eyes when he discovered we were literally surrounded by hundreds of rats. Yet, he managed to stay calm and enough not to spook them. I reached over and put my hand over Bubba's mouth, then nudged him. When he opened his eyes, I motioned for him to be still. We didn't even attempt to roll up our bags. We stood up very slowly. The rats closest to us hissed, and then scurried off into the high weeds. But the rest didn't seem concerned by our presence at all. We grabbed our bedrolls and packs and walked backwards dragging them out. Once out of the weeds, we rolled up our bags and then packed up. We all had a bad case of the willies over the whole ordeal.

"We've been asleep for about three hours," Al whispered. "It's time to look for our train".

While crossing between the W.P. and the S.P. yards, Al said that he saw a glimpse of a vehicle partially hidden in the shadows, about a hundred yards down the service road from us.

"Run like hell," he shouted.

In an attempt to make a run for it, we rolled under a couple of strings of cars and then scrambled over a couple more rows, before we heard gravel flying from a vehicle slamming on the brakes out on the service road.

"Hurry up and climb the ladder of this boxcar," said Al. Bubba climbed up first, as far as he could, then me, and then Al.

Moments later we heard static brake over on a walkie talkie when the dick climbed out of his vehicle. Then he got down on the ground and shined his flashlight beneath the cars. Moments later, we heard him climbing over strings of cars, coming our way. My heart pounded so loud inside my throat, I was sure he'd heard it when close enough.

"Be ready to bolt," Al whispered.

We were getting ready to make a run for it when we heard another vehicle stop out on the gravel road.

"Hey, Gary," someone shouted. "What are you doing back there?"

"Checking something out; thought I saw a couple guys duck into the yard.

"Come on its break time."

"The hell with it," said the dick, "they're probably long gone by now anyway."

I breathed much easier when I heard him climbing back over the cars.

We stayed on the ladder until we were sure he was long gone.

"I thought we were busted," Al said. "Let's find our train and get the hell out of here? This yard is hotter even, than I thought."

The first empty boxcar we found, we climb inside until we figured out what we were going to do.

"This car is sitting on an outbound track," he said, but I'm not sure of its destination."

"I've got a bad feeling about this yard," I said. If this is an outbound maybe we should stay put and hope for the best."

"You might be right," Al agreed. "It'll be getting light soon."

"Sounds good to me," Bubba yawned.

So we rolled out and were soon all back to sleep.

Chapter 17

"We're in the Oakland yard," I heard Al shouting and there won't be another train out of here, until later tonight."

I burrowed down inside my bag in hopes I'd wake up and find out it was all a bad dream. Then I got the idea; if there wasn't another train due to depart that yard until later in the evening, the kid and I could possibly spend the day in San Francisco.

"Bubba get up," I said. "We're goin' to San Francisco."

"Can I sleep a little longer," he whimpered.

"Sure sleep as long as you want, but I'm goin' to San Francisco."

I never saw him move so fast. After we were packed, I asked Al if he wanted to go along. He declined, he was afraid we might not make it back in time. But he gave me directions to a jungle he'd be waiting for us at in the area, in case we did make it before the train pulled out. We said our farewells just in case.

Eventually, Bubba and I managed to find our way out of thick the maze of railcars, and then out onto a public sidewalk. We stopped an elderly man and asked if he knew how to catch the bus across the Bay Bridge, over to the city. He then proceeded to tell us in great detail on what bus to take and where we were could catch it. We thanked him, then took off the find the bust stop.

Bubba's face was plastered against window as the bus crossed over the Bay Bridge. The view of the Oakland switchyard was impressive from the bridge. The yard seemed to go on for miles. Many of the tracks were occupied with Amtrak railcars.

After the bus dropped us off in downtown San Francisco, we walked over to the Greyhound bus depot, to store our gear in a locker, so we'd be free to enjoy the day.

In the process of stuffing our gear into to a locker, a man walked up and asked if we needed help with our baggage.

"No thanks!" I said, "Now shove off!"

"He was only trying to help," Bubba said.

"Help my ass. That's the oldest trick in the book. He slips ya another key and keeps yours. After you're gone, he doubles back and cleans out your locker."

"Why that sSon of a bitch!"

"Let's catch the trolley and ride it down to Fisherman's Wharf?"

"Yeah, let's go to Fisherman's Wharf!"

The fool kid hung off the front of the trolley, yeehawing like a lunatic the entire ride to Fisherman's Wharf. He really got a thrill when we helped turn the trolley around on a turn table to go back the other direction.

There couldn't be more of a perfect day to embark upon an adventure in San Francisco, I thought as I gazed out at Alcatraz Island framed in a cloudless cobalt backdrop. The air was crisp and clear with very low humidity and not a cloud was in sight. We checked out an old sSchooner docked at the water front, but there was free to tour it. Then we peered out at Alcatraz Island through a telescope that only cost a quarter. Afterwards we ran from place to place. Bubba was exuberant with excitement.

On the waterfront I bought us each a serving of clam chowder servered inside an edible sour dough bread bowl. We sat on a dock, enjoying our lunch, while watching Sea Lions play in the water.

After lunch, we rough and tumbled out on the in the waterfront park lawn until exhausted. Then we jumped back on a trolley rode it up to the "Trolley Museum," up on top of Nob Hill, on Clay Street, because a local had told us the museum was an icon of San Francisco and it was a must to check out if we were touring the city. Inside the museum, we read historical information about the earth quake that caused the fire, almost destroying the great city, in April, 18, 1906. We were also amazed to find out how the cable system worked. Apparently it kept moving 24/7, 365 beneath the city. The only time it was ever shut down, was to perform maintenance every so often on the cables, mainly after they'd been stretched out. I guess it was only then the system was shut down to shorten the cables. Hung on the walls were dozens of pictures of the old city, before it was rebuilt. Each photo had a footnote below, with tidbits of information about the history of the great city.

Later we got back on the trolleys and rode them on every foot of track they covered in San Francisco. That took better than c couple of hours.

"It's always been a dream of mine to see the Golden Gate Bridge," Bubba shouted, while hanging of the front of a trolley car.

After we had ridden the trolley the entire area it covered, we took city transportation out to Golden Gate Park. When we stepped off the bus, Bubba's mouth dropped wide open, as he stood in total awe, while gazing out at the famous renowned Golden Gate Bridge, glinting under the afternoon sun like a jeweled treasure. He didn't say a word for quite some time. Then he wanted to run down the steep bank to the waters edge. But I wouldn't let him. Later he got a wild notion we should become blood brothers when a freighter passed beneath the bridge.

"Are you sure you want to do this?"

"Damn right."

I pulled my pocketknife out, and then attempted to sterilize it with matches. Afterwards, we cut slits in our palms with it. Afterwards, we grasped a hold of each other's hands, while we watched the freighter steam out into the open sea. We stayed that way until the freighter vanished on the horizon. It had been an incredible day to say the least. But my gut feeling told me it was time we headed back to the Oakland yard.

"We've got a train to catch," I said breaking the silence.

The sun dipped below the horizon, drenching the bay in a golden splendor while our bus crossed the Bay Bridge.

What an awesome way to top off a perfect day, I thought as we gaped out across the sun-splashed bay.

When Al saw us approaching the jungle, a broad smile crossed his face

"Didn't think I'd see you boys again," he laughed. "An eastbound is already made up. No power yet, but it won't be long."

Al broke camp, then we threaded through the corridors until we found the track our train was made up on. It didn't take long to find an open Southern Pacific boxcar with both doors open. So we swung up inside and waited. Bubba had rolled out his bedroll and was fast asleep before the train ever departed. Shortly after he fell asleep the train eased out of the Oakland yard. Many thoughts bounced around inside my head, while I sat in the boxcar door. I hoped we'd be lucky enough to catch a train that'd take us all the way down into southern California. Eventually, I stretched out on my bedroll. A clanging railroad crossing startled me awake. I sat up and looked around. It was pitch black inside the car again. I was incoherent and just wanted to go back to sleep. Then I noticed Al sitting next to the door.

"We're coming into the Roseville yard," he said. "We made better time than I had hoped. There should be a southbound pulling out in the next couple of hours. I plan on being on it. If you boys are coming with me, you and the kid need to get ready."

It took a minute to register. But I was all for catching a southbound that night, the sooner the better.

"Yeah we're going with ya," I said groggily. I'll get the kid up."

I rousted him and told him get moving. He sat up and looked around rubbing his eyes.

"All right, I'm getting up," he snarled.

Once again we found ourselves in the Roseville yard. In the last couple of days we had gone from there, to Marysville, to Stockton, Oakland, and then back to Roseville.

Still half asleep Bubba and I followed Al until we reached the track he was looking for. Then we bubba and I walked on one side of the train and Al on the other. The first empty we came to, we climbed in. Then we all three rolled out in the front of the car and went back to bed.

The train was flying down the track so fast and the wheels were screeching so loud, I was having a tough time staying asleep. I didn't want to get out my bedroll, but Mother Nature called, forcing from the warmth of the old down sack. I jumped up and staggered towards the door. The train was clipping along so swiftly, it was difficult to walk without hanging onto the side of the car. After relieving myself, I sat down in the doorway to let the cool California night air wash over me. A few minutes later, I saw Bubba in the shadows making his way toward the door.

"Surprised to see you up," I said over the racket.

"I got woke up and had to pee, because the train is beating me up so bad and I now I can't get back to sleep."

"I know the feeling. "

"Pee on the other side of the door before we both end up with a shower," I said in a panic."

"Yeah, I almost forgot, Bubba said still half out of it. Afterwards, he sat next to me cross-legged in the doorway.

"You never did tell me about your dad," I said.

"Do you two get along ok?"

"We're a lot closer since he quit drinkin'. He used to drink so much, he started having health problems. Finally, the doctors told him if he didn't stop, he wasn't gonna be around much longer. That must have scared him enough to quit. As far as I know, he's been sober for over two years now. Before then, he was kind of mean and irritable most of the time. Now he's like a different person. He's only forty two, and has already had two heart attacks."

"I remember you mentioning his heart wasn't so good."

"His liver is in pretty bad shape too. His drinki'n' is what broke him and my ma up. Ma has family back in Yakima, that's how we ended up there. At least, I get to go stay with him through the summer months.   Ma and I were doing fine until hooked up with that no good sSon of a bitching Earl," he said through clinched teeth.

"Because of the circumstances, when you get to your dad's, I hope you'll be able to live with him permanently. Sounds like this Earl character really screwed your mom up pretty bad.

"I want to kill 'iem," Bubba snarled.

"I hope so. I'll be a hell of a lot happier with him, that's for sure. He takes me fishing a lot when I'm there in the summer. We do a lot of cool father and son things together since he quit drinking."

"Ever meet any hot babes while rambling up and down these railroad tracks?" asked Bubba.

"There was this one girl in Los Angeles. I still think about her often.

We were only together one night. But it was one of the most memorable nights of my life."

"Tell me all the juicy details," Bubba said with excitement.

"It's not as romantic as it sounds." I had caught a westbound Union Pacific train out Salt Lake City, bound for Los Angeles. My intention was to bail off in the big rail yard just outside of Barstow. But I fell asleep and woke up in LA. The yard in LA is in the roughest side of town. While walking down Hollywood boulevard, I witnessed a woman being beat by her pimp. By then, I had already heard gunshots and sirens wailing. I even witnessed kids younger than you selling their bodies to the scumbags of the night. By then, I was so terrified of losing my life; all I wanted to do was get the hell out of there. But I was dead broke and filthy from riding trains.

"What the does that have to do with romance," Bubba blurted out.

"I was getting around to that. Like I said before you interrupted, as I was crossing a street, a hot looking hooker asked if I wanted a date. I told her I was flat broke. Let me tell ya, she was beautiful too. She must have felt sorry for me, because she asked if I'd go home with her. At first, I was suspicious she might be some psycho killer. But when I gazed into her eyes, I knew she was sincere. She said business was slow, so she was gonna call it a night. Then she hailed down a cab. On the way to her apartment she told me her real name was Mary Jane and she was from Indiana. She got excited when I told her I was from Michigan.

To my surprise, her apartment was very neat and tidy. There were also hundreds of books on shelves that covered most of the walls. We talked for a while before turning in for the night. I was ready to sleep on the couch, when she said she'd prefer I sleep with her. We clung in each other's arms and talked and talked all through the night, as though we'd known each other our entire lives. It was dawn before we finally fell asleep.

"Well did ya do it," Bubba blurted out.

"Sorry to disappoint ya kid. It wasn't like that. She and I were both starved for someone to hold and someone to listen. Neither of us acexcepted anything in return. The next day we lay in bed, embracing in each others arms until it was time for her to go back to work. But before she went back to the street, she had the cab take me over to the Greyhound bus depot. Then she gave me fifty bucks to buy a ticket. I didn't want to take her money, but she acted hurt because I didn't want it. I took it. We hugged and kissed. Then I told her I was going to give up the road and I would come back for her. She swore that she'd give up hooking if I did come back. Then we could start a life together. But when we looked into each other's eyes, she knew I'd never give up the road, as she'd never give up hooking. I've never seen her since. But I still think about the incredible night we spent together more times than not."

"I can't believe you didn't tear that stuff up. Are you stupid or something?"

"Believe me, when I tell you that I was more than tempted. I didn't pursue it because I was afraid she might have been looking at her watch, if ya catch my drift. That's my story and I'm stickin' to it."

Just then the car flooded with light and a wisp of diesel smoke rolled into in to the car as a northbound screamed past the door. A few minutes later more lights flooded the car and clanging railroad crossing lights zinged past, when the train screamed through the town of Chowchilla.

We stayed up and talked for a while quite some time before we decided to try and get more shuteye.

CHAPTER 18

Al woke us up on the outskirts of Bakersfield and told us to hurry up and get ready, because we were gonna to have to bail on the fly.

Just after we rolled into the Bakersfield yard, we bailed off and then walked down to the departure yard, which was a good mile down the track. We sat beside a track where Al said our train would be made up on and waited while the train was being remade. As soon as we got there Bubba crawled back into his bedroll and slept through all the loud crashes and bangs that carried over from the hump yard.

"What are you doing out here," I asked Al. Let's just say you're not the average hobo.

"I'm a hobo, alright," he chuckled. "But I'm a gambler, a card player by profession. Lady luck hasn't been kind to me lately. So I needed to get away to clear my head. But, I've been running up and down these old railroad tracks since before you were born."

I enjoyed Al's easy going disposition. He seemed to be a very intelligent man. Although I'd only known him for a short time, I had already begun to have a great deal of respect and admiration for him.

"I'm worried about Colton."

"What do you mean," I asked.

"At times it can take a couple of days to catch out of there. The yard is hot and well patrolled, meaning we'll have to catch out off railroad property, under the bridge. A rough crowd hangs out there. I'm worried for the kid's sake."

"I've never caught out of there before, but heard plenty of stories how tough it can be."

"We'll have to keep a sharp eye for the kid."

176

"Trust me; he can handle himself in a tough spot."

"He is a cocky little guy, isn't he? But he's got grit. I'll give him that."

"Is that what you call it?," I laughed.

Our journey was definitely going to be more perilous from then on. After Colton, we still had Yuma, and El Paso to deal with. Both yards could be perilous at times, because they were border towns. After Indio the kid and I would be on our own again. I felt much safer being with Al. Though I knew my way around the rails fairly well, Al knew them far better than I ever would. For the first time since we'd departed Yakima, I had doubts if I'd done the right thing by taking the kid by freight-train. From then on we were gonna have to sleep with one eye open.

A yard dog, rumbled past pulling a long string of cars behind, breaking my concentration.

"Come on," Al said. "Let's go to Indio."

We woke the kid, and then made our way over to the track and started walking toward the rear. Bubba and I walked on one side, Al on the other. It didn't take long to find an open Missouri Pacific Boxcar, only on our side. The door on Al's side was closed shut. Al he crossed over, then we swung up inside and all went back to bed. Our train pulled out of the Bakersfield yard just at the break of dawn.

CHAPTER 19

When I woke Al and Bubba were standing next to each other with their heads hanging out the door hooting and hollering about something. Then Al did a jig across the boxcar floor.

"What's goin' on?" I asked in the middle of a yawn.

"The train is by passing Colton altogether and goin straight onto Indio," Al said "that's what's going on."

Since Al was getting off in Indio, I figured it would be as good as place as any to try and pick up a day's work. Most of the money I'd made back in Marysville was already spent.

Later the three of us sat in between the open doors cross-legged and shared pretty much the rest of our food, while we watched cactuses and Joshua Trees zing past.

"Is there any work in Indio?" I asked.

"There's no guarantee the train will even stop there. Most do, but not all. If that's the case, we'll have to hitch it back from Yuma over to Indio. If a guy wants to work bad enough, he can always scrape up something to do there."

"That's all I needed to hear. Like a moron, I blew most of our money back in Frisco."

Later that afternoon our train rolled in to Indio. Although it didn't stop, it slowed plenty enough for us to bail off on the fly.

"You're in my stomping ground now boys," Al said cheerfully.

We bailed off then Al took us to a jungle down the tracks a ways.

Luckily for us, the previous tenants left a pile of broken up pallets for burning. We immediately started a fire and got the last of our coffee on.

After the sun dipped behind the horizon, the evening sky exploded with a multitude of brilliant colors and the cry of coyotes sang out across the desert. While we sat around campfire, Al shared some incredible stories with us about his life and times of being a gambler. He told us about some near death predicaments he'd managed to get himself into, through the years, with people who were sore losers. By the time he'd finished, I couldn't keep my eyes open anymore. So I stretched out under a blanket of stars, while listening to Al and Bubba sharing time together.

When a westbound bound freight rumbled past, I sprung up and scanned the eastern sky. The glow of dawn was already on the horizon. I It was time to get moving if I was to score any work. Al had told me the night before, the best place to find day labor work in Indio was at the Rescue mission. He said for me wait around out front until someone pulled up and asked for help. I jumped up, threw on some clothes and then scurried away.

There were at least twenty men milling around out front when I got there and hope seemed bleak. A few minutes later a red pickup truck pulled up front. A big hulk of a man, built like a pro linebacker, stepped down out of his four wheel drive pickup. I watched him walk around the front the vehicle. He had a mean look upon his face.

Then someone nudged me and said that he was pointing at me. A few of the locals grumbled as I made my way through the crowd.

"My name's Mike," I said, extending my hand.

"People call me Buck." Then he reached out his huge callused paw and shook my hand.

"You're a pretty good sized old boy, any good at organizing?".

"Whatever you need done, I can do it."

"That's the attitude I like to hear. I have a big ole pole barn out behind my house that needs to be reorganized in the worst way. There's so much crap inside, I can barely move around anymore. I'll show you what I want done when we get there."

Then I jumped into the passenger seat.

When we arrived at his spread, he led me to the barn, explaining what he wanted done. Then he showed me how he wanted the job completed and how he preferred things to be organized. I was overwhelmed at first and wanted to run away. But after we stacked some old scrap metal, moved around a couple of piles of lumber and moved an old dust covered vehicle, I saw light at the end of the tunnel. Then Buck told me that he needed to run a few errands in town and he'd be back in a couple of hours. By then, I was confident enough to know what and how he wanted things done. After he'd left, I dug in and started making some serious headway.

What seemed like only a few minutes later, Buck walked back into the barn with a Mc Donald's bag in his hand.

"It's lunch time," he said, then he handed me a couple of Big Mac's, a large order of fries, and a Coke. I was so hungry; I could have eaten an entire cow.

"Thanks!"

"Just glad you appreciate it. Nothing pisses me off more than when I do something for someone and they don't appreciate it."

Buck reminded me of my dad. He didn't look anything like him, just more the way he perceived things.

"You're a hard worker, and seem as though you're a good kid. What the hell are you doing rambling around the countryside like a nomad for?"

"I'm cursed with the wander lust. I can't seem to stay any one place very long."

"Wander lust, my ass," he blurted out. What you need is a trade. I'm in the sign business," he said boastfully. "And I make an excellent living at it too, if I don't say so myself. You need to find yourself a trade and then settle down with a good woman like mine. I couldn't ask for a better wife. She keeps a clean house, and has been a wonderful wife and always and an great mom to our sons."

"How many kids do you have?

"Two sons, twenty five and twenty two."

"Where are they now?"

"College, where you should be," Buck said sternly.

"Yeah, you might be right. I've got friends I went to school with who are in college. Maybe someday I'll go myself, if I ever shake these rambling railroad blues."

"The fact that we're all different makes the world go around," Buck said on a kinder note. "I suppose it's time to get back to work. I've got some things to do around the house. You mind taking over the helm?"

"No problem. Do your thing, while I get the barn in shipshape skipper."

"I believe you will," he laughed.

I tore back into the project the moment he left, because I wanted to get as much done as possible, assuming he'd want me to come back and finish up the next day. Not that we couldn't use the money, I just didn't want to leave the kid alone any more than I had to.

I got so involved in putting things in the right piles, tidying up, and sweeping floors, I completely lost track of the time.

Buck walked up behind me and said, "Hot dog, it doesn't look like the barn anymore. But it's time to call it a day. It's near five o'clock. Son, you just put in a ten hour day. I hope you're hungry, the little woman has got a hot home cooked meal waiting for you on the table."

I really felt the need to get back; mainly because I was worried about the kid. But it had been a while since I'd had a home cooked meal. Besides, if I were to decline, I'd only hurt his feelings. Maybe even down right piss him off. The last thing I wanted was upset after the kindness he'd shown me.

"You don't have to ask me twice," I said.

Buck's wife was tall and slender woman, with a very pretty youthful face, and she was very much a lady.

Supper consisted of, pork-chops, mashed potatoes, gravy, fresh green beans, and peach cobbler. The chops were succulent and tender, and at least an inch thick. The peach cobbler was still hot and topped with a scoop of vanilla ice cream.

After dinner Buck and I stepped outside and sat down on top of his picnic table and threw back a couple of cold ones. Coyotes sang to the coming night, and whining tires of eighteen wheelers echoed from the nearby highway. Buck was in the mood to talk. It was apparent he missed his sons.

"Mike, if you'd stick around, I'd teach you the business and make you my apprentice. My sons don't want anything to do with it."

"Why would you do something like that," I asked. "You don't know me from Adam."

"Maybe not, but I pride myself being a good judge of character. You're a good kid, I just know it. I just don't want you to throw your life away. In the little time I've spent with you, I can see that you have potential to do great things if you were to put your mind to it."

I was moved by his confidence in me. But I knew if I were to try to explain to him what I was doing, he'd never be able to grasp it.

"I appreciate what you're saying," I said with humbleness. "Not in my entire life has any one ever spoken as kindly as you have tonight. You've treated me more like a son, instead of the two bit drifter I really am. But as we speak, there's a fifteen year old boy waiting for me at the mission. I took an oath to get him back to Dallas, Texas and have been trying to get him there ever since. I took him under my wing back in Yakima, Washington because he'd been thrown out into the street like trash by his mother's abusive, alcoholic boyfriend like trash. Your offer is an opportunity of a life time. I might surprise you and come back and take you up on it. But for now, I've got an important mission to complete. The kid is depending upon me to get him home safely. If I told you half the things we've already been through together, you probably wouldn't believe me."

There was a long pause of silence. "I respect what you're doing," Buck said. And I admire your courage. This only tells me I'm right about you. After you get this kid home, I hope you'll seriously consider my offer. I think we'd make a good team."

"Thanks for understanding," I said.

"Well, I guess I best get you back."

Big Al and Bubba stepped out of from the shadows when Buck's truck pulled up in front of the mission. Bubba ran up to the side truck.

"I knew you'd come back," he said.

"Buck, this is Curtis, the kid I was telling ya about."

"Nice to meet you son," Buck said as he extended his hand out to shake.

"You do what Mike tells you and I believe you'll get home just fine."

"Yes sir," he said with a wide grin.

"And this is Al. Al has helped us get through some tough spots along our journey."

"Nice to meet you too Al," Buck said, extending his hand again.

"Oh yeah," I almost forgot." He opened his wallet and handed me a fresh crisp fifty dollar bill. I was speechless.

"Thank you," I said almost in tears.

"The same to ya Mike," said Buck. Take good care of that kid and be careful out there you hear. I hope to see you soon. Then he gunned it, flinging gravel and dust as he disappeared into the desert blackness.

"What do you say we head back over to the jungle and call it a night?" Al suggested.

It was already after nine o'clock. I was exhausted. I didn't feel much like riding trains, especially through Yuma, in the middle of the night. Actually, I preferred to go through there in the light of day.

"I'm all for that. After working all day, I'm too tired to go anywhere tonight."

"All right," Bubba said, disappointed.

"I know you're anxious to get goin, but Yuma, Arizona is no place to be messing around in the middle of the night. Sometimes the trains break up there, meaning we'd have to catch another one. Most of the people who come across the border are desperate."

"Okay, okay, he snapped, "I get it."

On the way to the jungle, we stopped off at an all night grocery. There I picked up a few odds and ends for the road. It broke my heart to break that crisp new fifty dollar bill. I handed Al a ten spot.

"You and the kid are going to need this," he protested, while trying to stuff the bill in my shirt pocket.

"If you don't take it, I'll consider it as an insult."

"All right, have it your way kid. I can use it."

"Good, then it's a done deal."

While sitting around the campfire, Al shared more gambling tales with us. I listened until I couldn't keep my eyes open any longer. The last thing I remembered was a westbound freight rumbling past the jungle.

CHAPTER 20

When an eastbound freight rumbled past, dawn had already begun to spread across the eastern horizon. Eventually, the train came to a loud a screechy stop. But when it did, the caboose was at least a couple hundred yards up the track from the jungle. Bubba and I threw our belongings together and then woke Al to say goodbye and thanked him many times for helping us along Bubba's homeward journey.

"You best get moving," he said groggily. "Before that train starts moving."

Bubba and I slung our packs over our shoulders, and then took off running for the train in the pre-dawn light.

"Boys be careful out there you herear!," Al shouted as we jogged down the service road toward the train.

Al, I hope our paths cross again someday," I yelled back.

I was having a hard time keeping up with the kid because I was so sore from working the day before. About twenty cars up past the caboose, we approached an open boxcar. Suddenly a man poked his head out the open door.

"If you plan on riding this here train, ya better get' in with us, because' it's the only open car on it."

I was leery about riding with people I didn't know. Once the train was in motion you'd have no choice but to stick it out. But we tossed our gear in anyway, and swung up inside. We had barely got settled in the back of the car when the train eased forward.

There were three other men sitting in the front of the car passing a bottle of wine. At first, I panicked, because Bubba and I were now trapped on a moving car with four strangers we had no idea of who they were. But through time on the road, I had acquired a keen sixth sense about people, and could usually tell if they had evil on their minds. My gut told me everything was going to be ok. So I walked over to where all four men were sitting in a circle and said:

"I'm Free Bird and this here is Bubba Lee, out of Texas."

The older tall lanky man that had greeted us at the door stood up, "I'm Wing Nut," where ya boys off to?"

"Dallas, Texas said Bubba.

"Well I'll be. The four of us is goin' thru the Big D ourselves. From there we're all goin' to my place in Arkansas. You're welcome to come along if ya like. The more the merrier."

Then another man said: "They call me the Pennsylvania kid, he slurred.

"I'm Hobo Joe," said another man.

"I'm Texas Bob," said the fourth.

My gut instinct was right. These were just some good old boys traveling together and not out to hurt anybody. Besides, I already felt more at ease about passing thru Yuma and El Paso with a group, than just the kid and me alone.

Bubba and I sat in the doorway and watched Joshua Trees and Cactuses zip past while the train motivated out across the open desert.

We rolled into Yuma around ten in the morning. We weren't sure if it the train was going to break up so we sat there and waited to hear if the engines were going to break air. A good hour past and we still didn't hear anything. In that time at least a couple of dozen illegal Mexican's had tried to get on the car with us, bBut Wing Nut ran back and forth between the two doors and greeted them with his Smith & Wesson .38 special. The moment they saw the gun, they kept on stepping down the line and didn't look back. The train finally pulled out just before noon. We all breathed easier once we were on the move again.

Somewhere between Tim buck two and hell on earth, the train pulled into a siding. An hour passedt, then another and still another, the entire time, the unmerciful sun beat down upon the metal roof of the boxcar. Within a couple hours the inside of the car was so unbearable that we couldn't even stand to sit on the floor. And it just kept getting hotter and hotter the longer we sat. We couldn't dare touch our water bottles without scorching our mouths.

"It must be a hundred and fifty degrees in here," Bubba groaned.

"If this train sits here much longer, our brains is gonna cook," Wing Nut said.

"Do ya have any suggestions," Pennsylvania Slim asked.

"Yeah but ya ain't gonna like it," said Wing Nut.

"Tell us," Texas Bob growled. "Anything's better than sittin in here and getting our brains cooked."

"What if we were to climb beneath the car? Then it would become shade to us instead. You gittin' my drift."

"What the hell are we supposed to do if the train starts movin'?" said Texas Bob. But maybe it's dumb enough to work."

While listening to the two of them bicker back and fourth, I thought how they reminded me of an old married couple.

"I'm willing to risk it," chimed in Bubba.

"Me too," I agreed.

"What if we set our gear next to us?" I said. That way if the car so much as flinches, we'll scramble out from underneath and hope for the best."

"Why don't we leave it sitting in the doorway," Wing Nut suggested.

"That way if the car moves we should be able to pull our gear off in time."

It was agreed to do just that. So we stacked everything in a heap in the doorway. Then we squatted down underneath the car. Wing Nut was right. The moment we crawled beneath the car the air becameand semi- bearable. We sat back to back inside the rail, in three pairs. I warned Bubba not to get too comfy, because it was a vital we be ready in a flash if the train were to start moving. We all must have looked pretty ridiculous sitting underneath the grungy old boxcar.

"I'm so thirsty," Bubba whimpered, I could drink a lake.

"That makes two of us." "At least everything will cool down after the sun sets."

"Do you think we'll be here that long?" Bubba groaned

"I hope the hell not. No pun intended" That made him laugh.

"Look," Bubba said pointing. There's some a crazy ass dog walking around out there."

"That's no dog, ninny, that's a coyote."

"I knew that," he said.

"Yeah, whatever. What was I thinking? A Texan is never wrong."

The poor coyote staggered around like a drunkard, with its tongue lulling out of its mouth. At least Wing Nut entertained us with funny stories about his misadventures of his life out on the road. After what seemed like eternity the blistering sun finally slanted over toward the horizon. By then we were all so stiff, none of us could have ever been able get back on the train before it started to move if our lives depended on it. We scrambled from beneath the car, then we all climbed back inside. We were just thrilled to be able to get back in the car and stretch out again.

The train finally pulled out of the siding just after dark. We all cheered and gave each other high fives.

"I can honestly say that that was the closest to hell, I've ever come," Wing Nut chuckled.

It was at least another hour before we were on the move again. Soon we saw dozens of vehicles and cranes. People were walking around on both sides of the track and the entire area was lit up as bright as day with lighs on poles. Apparently there had been a derailment. Freight and debris was scattered all along the tracks for a long way. Off to the side were three boxcars bent and twisted like Tonka Toys. It was only then that we understood why we had sat out in the desert for so long, and hadn't seen a single oncoming train either. None of us said a word until the wreck was long behind us.

We all knew that could have easily been us on one of those cars.

"It's a miracle only three cars jumped the track," Wing Nut said, breaking the silence. "It could have been much worse."

We finally rolled into Tucson somewhere around midnight. Wing Nut and the gang decided they were jumping off in Tucson, because their beer had been ruined from the intense heat. So I decided we'd get off the train with them. I wanted to get cleaned up, eat a hot meal, and do some laundry anyway. Even Bubba thought it was a good idea. I think our ordeal in the desert flat took the wind out of everybody's sails.

We camped out in a park near the tracks. No one was in the talking mood. Plus it was against regulations to build a fire within the park limits anyways. So we all rolled out and went to straight to bed. Before long I was being lulled to sleep by a chorus of snorers and gas explosions on both sides of me.

CHAPTER 21

No one made an attempt to get up until the scorching morning sun drove us from our bedrolls.

While Bubba and I were sitting on a bus stop bench at the bus stop, waiting for our transport to pick us up, the realization of us parting roads hit me like a hard. I don't think he was going to miss me as much as I was going to miss him.

When the bus driver opened the door cool air gushed out to greet us. We sat directly in front of an air duct and pulled the cool air in toward us with our hands. The bus driver kept looking back at us in his mirror, as though we were a couple of freaks. You never know just how much you appreciate the small things in life until you've gone without. We had had our share of going without a great many things in the last couple of weeks.

We stashed our gear in a locker at the Greyhound bus depot, except for a change of clean clothes. Afterwards we walked over to an old hotel Wing Nut had told us where we could to sneak in and clean up. While the kid went around the back, I walked through the lobby. The man behind the counter didn't even look up. I went straight to the back door and opened it to let the kid in. However, the old hotel didn't have showers, so we had to take turns in a dirty old tub. Just the same it felt good to be clean again.

From the hotel we caught a bus over to a smorgasbord restaurant. I almost had tears in my eyes when I saw all that food spread out before us. The buffet consisted of succulent roast-beef, seafood, chicken and so much more. There were also dozens of trays of deserts and an ice-cream machine to boot. We had over a dozen plates stacked up in a pile and were just finishing up with desert when the manager walked past. We he noticed all the plates heaped in a stack, he gave us the evil eye of disapproval. We didn't care, neither of us could have eaten another bite anyway.

Outside the restaurant I told Bubba there was someplace special I wanted to take him to, and it was within walking distance.

Bubba beamed from ear to ear when he realized we were standing in front of an Army, Navy surplus store.

"This is what I wanted to show you."

"Bitchin!" he said with excitement.

When we stepped inside the strong odor of canvas was almost overwhelming. For the next couple of hours we checked out just about everything inside that store.

"Look Mike," Bubba said. These down bags are only sixteen bucks.

"These are what I wanted to show you. It still gets pretty damn cold on top of the pass outside of Lordsburg at night. This store has the cheapest mummy sacks I've ever found anywhere."

We rummaged through the pile of used bags until we found one that looked practically brand new. Then we found a small narrow stuff sack to go with the bag.

On the way back to the park Bubba asked me what he should do with his old sleeping-bag.

"If Wing Nut and the gang are still at the park when we get back, I think you should give it to Wing Nut. I bet he'd be glad to take it off your hands. All he has is a couple of raggedy old blankets. An important rule of the road is if someone gives you something. Give something in return."

"I'm gonna to miss the road," Bubba said with regret.

"Yeah, the road does have a way of getting into your blood doesn't it? When you're safe and cozy at home, in your warm bed, try to remember me once in a while would ya."

Sure enough the gang was still at the park when we got back. They were well on their way to getting wasted. In fact, they were already pretty wasted.

When the kid handed Wing Nut his old sleeping-bag, Wing Nut was speechless.

"Kid this means a helluva lotlva" to me," he said. I've been needin'a good bedroll for quite a spell now."

"Good," Bubba responded. "I hope you can get some good use out of it."

"I will kid, . Aand every time I climb into it, I'' will think of you."

Out of the blue, Bubba did a jig and yelped, "Let's go to El Paso."

"I'm all for that," said Wing nut. "But I think its best we catch out after dark. That damn Bull drives up and down those tracks, during crew changes, like a Gestapo agent. It's much easier in the dark, especialla' with a bunch of drunken fools like us."

Shortly after dark the whistle of an eastbound called out across the void like an old friend. A few minutes the train rolled in and then came to a loud squeaky stop. We packed up, then we crept down near the tracks and hid in the shadows, waiting for the dDick to make a sweep down the train with his spotlight. When he did, he actually helped us spot an open box that was only a few cars up from us. We crept toward the car in the shadows. Except for Wing Nut, the other three were stumbling and staggering like drunken sailors. We all dove for the ground as the Bull made another sweep. Then we ran toward the car and jumped in. After we were all inside, I breathed easier. Things seemed to be going our way. Both doors were wide open.

"Mike watch the other door, while I watch this one," Wing Nut said. "When ya see the dDick comin' we'll move to the other side of the car.

Wing Nut's plan was brilliant. Whatever direction the Bull came from, we moved from one side to the other. That way we were able to stay hidden out of his light. However, the process was much more difficult than it sounded. Organizing a bunch of drunks that thought the whole matter was quite hilarious was frustrating to say the least. We had to move back and forth a a couple two more times before the train finally pulled out.

Bubba and I sat in the doorway after the train was out away from the lights of Tucson. It was a beautiful night to take a ride out across the desert. The air was fresh and the night sky was loaded with stars.

"What are ya gonna to do when ya get home," I asked

"The first thing is, I'm gonna look up all my old girlfriends."

"Was your dream girl, back in Eugene, one of these gals," I laughed.

A clanging rail road crossing zinged past. The train was now flat screaming out across the desert.

Yee haw! We're kicking ass and taking names," I shouted. The train was clipping along so fast, the train was actually passing eastbound cars out on the near-bye interstate.

"Back in Eugene, I was dreaming about Josephine. She's a fine little thang'" he said smacking his lips. Of course, all Texas girls are fine as hell."

"Listen to you,' you're fifteen and you talk like you're Romeo or Don Juan."

The car flooded with light again when the engines of an oncoming train screamed past, followed by a blur rocking screeching cars.

"Check out that shooter," Bubba yelped.

"That was a good shooting star for sure."

We talked into the night about girls and fast cars and about all the things he was going to do when got back home to his dad's place. Finally when neither of us could keep our eyes open, we called it a night and rolled out at the back end of the car. The strong scent of sage was refreshing on the cool desert air swirling around inside the car.

"Goodnight," Bubba said as he snuggled down into his new goose-down mummy bag.

Another clanging railroad crossing flashed past the door.

"Sleep tight, kid, I'll see ya in a while." Then I burrowed down myself and fell prey to the rhythmic melody of the rumbling wheels beneath: Clickety clack! Clickety clack! Clickety clack!

CHAPTER 22

I jerked awake with the uncanny feeling that I was being watched in my sleep, only to find a dark shadow hovering over me. As my eyes adjusted, I realized it was Wing Nut.

"What the hell are ya doing?" I said groggily. You scared the hell out of me."

"We've been sittin' in a siding' on top of a mountain on the outskirts of Lordsburg fer' the last couple of hours now. We're gonna take a chance and jump down and make a fire. We was wonderin' if you'd throw us our gear if we can't get back on the train in in time."

"No problem," I said still half out of it.

They stacked all theire gear on the edge of the doorway and then jumped down. After they jumped down, they looked for anything that would burn. They gathered up a bunch of pieces of old railroad ties that were alongside of the track and started a fire. An unmerciful frigid wind howled through the open doors, giving me a chill down to my toes, while sitting in the doorway listening for the slightest sound of hissing in the lines. It had to be in the twenties or colder. That train sat on the top of that mountain for at least an hour after they got their fire going.

The moment I heard hissing in the line, I yelled for them to get back on the train. Surprisingly, they scrambled back into the car faster than I expected they would.

As the train descended off the side of the mountain, the inside of the car gradually grew warmer. Finally we all went back to bed, in hope of grabbing a couple more hours' before we rolled into El Paso.

It seemed like only a few minutes later when I heard Wing Nut rambling on about bailing off on the fly in downtown El Paso, because he didn't want to make the five mile hike from the Alfalfa yard.

When the train rolled into El Paso we were all packed and sitting in the doorway waiting doorway, in hope that the train would slow down enough for us to bail off. Bubba yelped out a couple of yee haws because he was so happy to be back in the great state of Texas. As the train glided along the edge of the Rio Grande River, I gazed out at all lights winking lights carpeting the hillsides of Old Mexico, on the other side. About a half mile outside of town the train finally slowed enough for us to make the jump. "Here we go again," said Bubba, as he dropped down like a pro. Then the rest of us followed behind him.

As we walked on a road that paralleled the river, we heard the constant splashing of people crossing the shallows from Mexico. Wing Nut led the way to a darkened place behind the mission. It seemed as good as any to crash.

"I guarantee ya, we won't be harassed here," He whispered. And it's nice and dark back here.

CHAPTER 23

Everybody was already up and milling around by the time I woke.

"It's about time you got up, sleepy head," Wing Nut said. Me and Bob and are gonna hit the Plasma Bank. We heard it pays fifteen bucks a pop for the first timer. We're plum outta of beer money.'"

"I'm gonna hit it myself," I yawned. I made fifty bucks back in Indio, California, helping a guy clean out his barn, and I'm already flat broke. You guys go on ahead. I'll be coming behind ya soon. Bubba had a tizzy fit when I told him he was going have to go with me when I went to the plasma bank. I wasn't about to let him out of my sight, it's wasn't uncommon for people to disappear down there, especially young kids. Besides, I trusted Wing Nut and Texas Bob, but I was still out on the other two."

"What am I going to do for over two hours"? He whimpered.

"Buck up! Shut up! And pack up. Were outta' here!"

On the way to the plasma bank, we detoured down an alley, and stopped behind a Mexican restaurant. Then I knocked on the back door.

"Now what are we doing?" Bubba snapped.

"I'm gonna try to get us something to eat."

"And how do you propose we do that?"

"That's where you come in. Someone told me about this place a while back. I've already been here once and they gave me something to eat that time. Tell em'em in Spanish that we're down and out, and hungry."

Just then the door opened and a pretty senorita poked her head out.

Bubba immediately rattled something off in Spanish. She said something back, and then closed the door. A couple of minutes later her, and another pretty lady came out with a couple of Styrofoam takeout containers. They were both crammed full of tortillas and burritos. They also had a gallon jar of water. Both women seemed tickled that Bubba spoke fluent Spanish. They doted over him like a couple of mother hens. We ate until stuffed. Then the kid rattled off a bunch more Spanish. Soon they were chattering back and forth. I understood enough to know that he was telling them about our incredible journey. Let's just say by the time we left, that silver tongued devil had charmed those pretty ladies to the point they were heart broken to see him go.

Droves of people were standing outside the Plasma Bank when we arrived. Inside, people were packed like sardines and it was so loud and chaotic, it was hard to hear myself think. I was worried if I'd even get processed before they closed. But one of the nurses assured me that I would. Then she took my name while instructing me in very broken English to sit down and wait to be called. A few minutes later the border patrol burst in, making a search through out the building for illegal immigrants. I never saw so many people scatter and disappear so fast. By the time the Border Patrol had left, the place was almost vacant, except for the people who worked there and the donors lying on the beds. Like magic in a couple of minutes, I was called up front and was being processed.

"I want to do this too," Bubba said out of the blue. "For once I want to make my own money."

It's doubtful if they'll even let you do it. But I won't knock you for trying."

When they asked for Identification, Bubba said he didn't have any, that he had lost it. They asked him how old he was. He said 18. That was good enough for them. They gave us small cups for urine samples. Once they detected we didn't have any terrible diseases, we were led to one of the beds and told to lie down and get comfy. Looking at all the people lying there with needles the size of railroad spikes in their veins, gave me second thoughts. I had a phobia of needles anyway. But we needed the money and it was the quickest way to get it. Bubba lay on the bed next to me with a terrified look on his face. As much as I wanted to bolt, I had to be strong. Besides, it was nobody's fault but mine. I had been utterly foolish with our money up until that point. Now it was time to pay the piper. Although I had donated plasma many times in the past, doing it still always made me cringe.

"Mike, I'm scared," Bubba whimpered.

"It's not as bad as it looks," I said attempting to put his mind at ease.

"Before you know it we'll be thirty bucks richer."

"Yeah I guess."

"Hang in there kid," Wing Nut said from a bed across from us.

"When we get out of here," put in Texas Bob, "we're all goin to Old Mehieco' and buy you a cold one."

"I'm not old enough," Bubba said with wide smile.

"You are over there," Bob said.

Bubba put on his bravest face, and said: "I'm a man now."

Just then a lady walked over to his bed with a basket in hand. Then she rubbed alcohol on his forearm and wrapped a piece of stretchy rubber hosing around his bicep. The kid looked a little peeked while she searched his arm for a good vein to poke. But not as peeked as I did when she poked him.

Wing Nut and Bob were about an hour ahead of us. Wing Nut shared funny stories, about his home back in Arkansas, and how he couldn't wait to get back there so he could fire up his homemade still. It got kind of quiet in there after him and Texas Bob were done. By then the kid and I were comfortable enough. T the needles in our arms didn't seem to bother us anymore.

When the lady behind the counter handed each of us fifteen bucks cash money, the kid smiled from ear to ear. They also gave us two new identification cards with our pictures and names on them. He was ecstatic with his new Identification, and because he'd made his own money for the first time on our journey. He walked out of that plasma bank standing a little taller to say the least.

Wing Nut and Texas Bob were waiting for us outside. From there we walked to the bus station and stuffed our gear into a couple of lockers. Then we took off for the border. On the way, the kid kept pulling out his picture I. D. out and gawking at it.

Customs only inquired about what our business was in Mexico, and how long we indented to stay. But they never did ask for identification.

Strung along the street were countless small shops and the smell of authentic Mexican food floated heavily on the breeze. Many children on the streets tried to sell us trinkets and such. As much as I wanted to help those cute little kids the minute we gave one of them a dime, we'd be swarmed by the rest making it even tougher not help all of them out.

We found a quaint little bar tucked away from the hustle and bustle. A pretty little senorita wearing short shorts showing the cheeks of her butt, asked us in broken English, what we'd like to drink.

"Four Budweiser's," Bob said.

She popped open four Longneck bottles of Budweiser and brought them over to our table.

"Let's drink to Bubba's safe return home," shouted Texas Bob.

Then we knocked our bottles together. The lady from behind the bar smiled, then went about her business. Bob bought the first round, then Marvin, then me, and then Bubba bought the fourth. The barmaid never even flinched when he paid for the drinks. As euphoria kicked in, Bubba began laughing hysterically about anything and everything someone said. It didn't matter what, he'd burst into laughter. Pretty soon we were all laughing and having a good time. It was funny to listen to the kid slur his words, and still try to act cocky at the same time. After four rounds, we decided it was time to head back and find the others who were waiting for us over in the Missouri Pacific switchyard.

Stepping back outside from the darkened cantina, we all squinted under the bright afternoon sun. Wing Nut suggested we stop at a liquor store so him and Bob couple pick up a couple bottles of Tequila before they crossed back over the border. They each purchased a bottle of authentic Tequila that had the worm in the bottom.

As we approached Customs, I warned Bubba to try and act sober. When they asked us if we had bought any goods in Mexico, Wing Nut and Bob showed them the two bottles of tequila.

"Ok," the man said, then took the next person in line.

As we walked toward the Missouri Pacific switchyard the warm southwestern blowing across from Old Mexico ruffled Bubba's curly locks. Suddenly it hit me how much he had grown since our paths had first crossed back in Yakima. The way he carried himself, the way he walked, even his facial expressions were different. Somewhere between Yakima and El Paso, he had blossomed into manhood. He was no longer the same boy I had met what seemed so long ago. I couldn't have been more proud of him. I laughed inwardly, remembering, how I was pulled into this gig kicking and screaming. All I wanted to do was get him home and out of my life as soon as possible. Now it pained me that we were on the final leg of our journey. At the same time I was happy for him. In a couple of days he'd be finally be returned home safely to his father.

"You ok?" Bubba said, breaking my thoughts. "For a minute you looked as though you were gonna cry."

"I'm fine. I was just thinking."

It was past seven o'clock by the time we were all settled into the jungle; in the Missouri Pacific Yard. Hobo Joe and the Pennsylvania kid already had a fire going and dinner started. I immediately slid the coffee pot onto the grid for Bubba and me. Hobo Joe had a batch of Polish sausage cooking in a pan.

After consuming his delicious dinner, Wing Nut broke out one of the bottles of the tequila. When he went to hand it to Bubba, I stopped him. Our venture over to Mexico was one thing. I didn't want the kid thinking it was ok to drink anytime he wanted.

"Look guys, we still had a train to catch," I said.

"He's right," Marvin agreed. "We should hold off until we're on the train. We don' need no trouble. Nobody usuala' bothers ya in this yard, but if a railroad worker was to see a bunch of drunks staggerin' around, he'd damn sure call the law. If I get caught with this gun, it'd be off to the gray-bar motel fer me." So we drank coffee and sat around the fire.

Later Wing Nut pulled out a harmonica from his pocket and played the song, "I've been everywhere," by Johnny Cash, while Texas Bob sang it with perfection. Then we all joined in. Afterwards they performed a few other old vintage railroad songs. There was a touch a magic in the air. Millions of stars veiled the night sky and the coyotes sang in harmony to the music. Watching the firelight dance in their eyes as they played on, stirred the gypsy deep within my soul. Once again I remembered why I loved the freedom of the road.

Our concert was abruptly broken up when two blue Missouri Pacific engines rumbled past out in the switchyard. Then they started making the train that would carry us on into Big Spring.

For the next couple hours we listened to the rumble of the engines working out in the yard and the booms of the cars following when smashing into each other. Around ten o'clock the train was finally made up and all was quiet once again. Then it was pulled it out onto the main track, ready for departure.

"Well men," Wing Nut said, "It's time to break camp and find somethin' to ride." We spotted a Missouri Pacific boxcar that had both doors wide open.

"I guess it don't get no better than this," said Texas Bob. From out of the silhouettes of several men were running toward the same car.

"Run for it," Wing Nut shouted.

We ran all ran like Jack Rabbits for the car. We reached it just before the rest of them did. Wing Nut shinned his flashlight inside to make sure no one else was already inside.

"It's empty," he said. Toss your junk inside and hurry up and git' in."

From out of nowhere three more guys ran up to the car. But when Wing Nut introduced them to Smith & Wesson, they backed off and went about their way.

"It might seem mean, what I'm doin'," Wing Nut said. "But when the border Patrol comes lookin' for 'em, and they will be before this train leaves, we'd be the ones in trouble."

Sure enough, a few minutes later we saw the Border patrol walking on both sides of the train with flashlights. When they came to our door they shinned in their lights in our faces and asked if we were all Americans. We were then asked to speak so they could listen for any accents. When satisfied, they moved on down the line. Not long after, our car jerked forward and we were on the move. Texas Bob pulled a tire knocker from his pack and stood in one of the doors, While Wing Nut stood in the other. After the car was moving, several more guys tried to run along side and get into with us, until Bob and Wing Nut showed them their attitude adjusters. Then they'd quickly fall away from the train. The boys kept watch until the train picked enough speed not to worry about anyone trying to get on. Finally they sat down and relaxed.

How invigorating it was to hear the mega horsepower locomotives scream out across the land.

"We're railroading now!," I shouted, as we picked up speed. Soon the steel wheels beneath were playing my favorite tune, Clickety clack! Clickety clack! Clickety Clack!

Bubba yelped, "I'm goin' home, I'm goin' home", then we high fived in the center of the car. Wing Nut and the others were more interested in making love to their bottles of tequila.

The kid and I sat in the doorway and gazed out at the millions of stars in the night sky and took in deep breaths of sage scented the warm desert air.

Bubba spoke of how much he missed his dad. It was plain to see he had a great love and respect for him. And for the first time since we'd left Yakima, he spoke of his mother, of how their lives went so bad after she'd met Earl. I was moved as he poured out his heart to me. He had been through too much and experienced more grief than any kid should ever have to endure. He was due for a break. While he poured out his heart to me, the towns of

Hancock, Mc Nary, and Sierra Blanca had past like a blur. On the west side of Van Horn, neither of us could keep our eyes open any longer.

By then Wing Nut and the rest of gang were all passed out in the front of the car. None of them were in their bedrolls and it was quite chilly inside the car, but I just let em'em bee. I figured they had plenty of antifreeze flowing inside their veins.

Bubba and I rolled out at the other end. The last thing I remembered was lights flooding the inside of car as an oncoming train rumbled past.

CHAPTER 24

When I woke Pennsylvania kid and Hobo Joe were standing bye the door talking to Wing Nut about bailing off the train if slowed down enough when rolling through Odessa. From what I could hear they wanted to try to find work in the oilfield, because they'd heard that some of the rigs in Odessa area were hiring hands. Wing Nut was trying to talk them into going the rest of the way to Arkansas with him and Bob. But their minds were made up.

I yawned and stretched and then jumped and poked my head out the door. As far as I could see were silhouettes of dew covered oil derricks and power lines glistening under the rising sun. It looked as though it were going to be another beautiful spring day as soon as the fog burned off. Hobo Joe and Pennsylvania kid promised Wing Nut they'd look him up as soon as they had some jingle in their pockets.

On the outskirts of Odessa the train did slow down plenty enough from them to bail off.

They said their farewells, then tossed theire gear out. Joe sat down in the door, grabbed as hold of the latch and then dropped. Then Pennsylvania dropped down behind Joe. Wing Nut and I craned our heads out the door and waved until their silhouettes vanished in the morning haze. I went to wake the kid. Surprisingly, he was already up.

"Where are we?" he asked groggily.

"We're just outside of Big Spring. When we get there you and I are goin' to the store to buy enough food to make a breakfast big enough for an army.

"Yeehaw!" he said smacking his lips and rubbing his belly. "I'm starving."

"You're always hungry."

"Sounds damn good to me," Wing nut chimed in.

Wing Nut led the way through the Big Spring switchyard, to a cozy jungle hidden in a grove of trees, near the front of the yard. There were already a pile of boards there from previous visitors. So I immediately started a fire and got the coffee pot on the grill. Before long the aroma filled the air, hHowever, it took some coordinating to prepare the food, because I only had two pans and Wing Nut and Bob didn't have any. However, Bubba I worked together as a team. Before long we were feasting on bacon and eggs, and blueberry pancakes. We all ate and pigged out until none of us could eat another bite.

"That was the best breakfast ever," Bubba said rubbing his stomach.

After breakfast, Wing Nut and Texas Bob walked into town to see if were eligible to receive food emergency food stamps. They asked me to go with them, but I knew the kid would never have the patience to wait around for a couple of days, being so close to home. Besides, I believed in working for what I got and taking care of myself. I didn't feel it was the Government's job to take care of me while I was gallivanting all around the country side, having adventures at their expense. After they'd left the kid and I stretched out against our packs, read and sipped coffee. I soon began to feel very drowsy as all that food settled. But before I dosed off, I sternly warned Bubba to stay out of mischief. He didn't even look up from his book. I wondered if he really didn't hear me, or was he ignoring altogether.

Then next thing I remembered hearing was Wing nut say something about a lady coming from the social services in a few minutes to check out the camp.

I sat up and yawned, "What are you rambling on about."

"I said the lady from social services is comin' to make sure we have utensils and a proper place to cook our food at. It might be best if take the kid disappear until she's gone."

"I agree," I said. If she sees the kid, there could be trouble."

Bubba and I strolled out into the yard and climbed up onto the platform a grain hopper, where we still had a view of the camp. A few minutes later a car pulled up near the camp. Then a woman got out of the vehicle and walked into the jungle. She was only there a few minutes, before we watched her drive away. Once her car was out of sight, Bubba and I climbed down out of the car and walked back to the jungle.

"Are ya boys goin' to catch out tonight?" asked Wing Nut.

"As far as I know," I said. The kid's anxious to get home."

"I can sure understand that."

"But, if Bob and I want to git' our food stamps, we have to hang out fer' a couple of days. Our case worker said she could git' us emergency stamps, but it'll take forty eight hours."

It was a straight shot from Big Spring to Dallas. It would have been nice to go to Marvin's place in Arkansas, but I couldn't see making the kid wait around a moment more than he had to. I planned on being on that train, hell or high water. At the same time I didn't want to appear ungrateful for Wing Nut's generous invitation. If Bubba sat around there for a two more days, he would have driven us all into the nut house.

The railroad crew started making up our eastbound train just after sundown. By then, Wing Nut and Texas Bob had been hitting the sauce pretty heavy and were both wasted. When the rumbling and crashes stopped Bubba and we got ready to make the final leg of his homeward journey.

"It looks like you guys are plannin' on catching out tonight," slurred Wing Nut.

"I'm afraid so my friend", I said. "Hopefully our paths will cross again soon. Thanks for watching out for Bubba and me. I'll never forget you, if by chance our paths don't to cross again."

"Here," Then he handed me a piece of paper with his address and instructions on how to get to his place in Arkansas on it. "If your ever in my neck of the woods don' be a stranger. It was good thang' you did takin' the kid under your wing. The good lord will bless ya for it son. Take care and be careful out there ya hear. Bubba if I ever catch ya riding these here rails, I'll kick yer' sorry ass all the way back to Texas. Ya hear me boy?."

"That goes for me to," said Texas Bob.

"I hear you," Bubba said sheepishly.

We said our farewells. Then we turned towards the switchyard. Actually it felt good to be on our own again. We hadn't been alone since Marysville, California. Bubba was silent as we walked towards the train, as though he had something on his mind. Going back to a normal life style was going to be an adjustment for him.

We had to walk pert near the entire length of the train before finding an empty car. I shined my flashlight inside to make sure there were no surprises, then we swung up inside. Not long after, we heard crashing cars coming our way, then we jerked forward. Bubba didn't run to the door and shout out the names of the logos like he usually did. He just sat in the front of the car with his head bowed. I stood in the door and watched the lights of Big Spring until they vanished on the horizon. After some coaxing, I was able to talk Bubba into moving near the door. We sat cross legged and cracked open a couple of sodas while watching the lights of Buford City zing past. By then, he was in better spirits begining to enjoy the ride. The train was flat making excellent time. But the tracks were so bad in spots; it felt as though the wheels were airborne at times.

"Let's try to stay up until we get to Dallas," Bubba said.

But we fizzled out just on the other side of Abilene. So we decided to crash out for a couple of hours, and then get back up. We stretched out our bags for our last time on the train together.

"I'll see you in a couple hours kid," I said. But there was so much bad track on the old Missouri Pacific line; it was tough to get any sleep. The car was jerking, squeaking, squawking and tossing so violently at times, it seemed as though it were going to take flight from the tracks at any given moment. And that concerned me, because that was exactly how those cars jumped the track back in Arizona. As I lay there bouncing, I prayed to the good Lord he spare us. Eventually the rumbling wheels beneath swept me away into broken dreams. Clickety clack, Clickety clack, Clickety clack. I woke to find that Bubba and I were literally skipping across the boxcar floor like a couple of jumping beans. The bounces were so fast and abrupt, no matter what I tried to break my arm free from my sleeping -bag; I couldn't. It was as though I was paralyzed. It was terrifying to lay there and watch Bubba and me bounce toward the open door like sacks of taters and couldn't do anything about it because neither of us could free our are arms from our bedrolls, and there was nothing to grab onto.

"Try to sit up," I shouted over the racket. But the more I tried to free my arms the worse it got. By then my feet were almost dangling over the side of the door. I braced myself for the expulsion, when the bouncing suddenly stopped.

"That was downright freaky," Bubba screamed as he rolled out of his bedroll.

"I've ridden many trains and nothing like that has ever happened to me before. In another few seconds we could have been ground up rail meat. After we pulled out all of our gear back to the front of the car, we made a solemn vow to never sleep with our arms inside our sleeping-bags for as long as we lived while on a moving train.

Bubba said that the bumpy ride had shaken the pee right out of him. When he poked his head out of the door, he said started yelping that he could see the lights of Fort Worth on the horizon.

"Yee haw, I'm finally home!"

I jumped up to check it out. Sure enough they shimmered on the horizon like diamonds. But,

I also noticed dark black clouds hovering above the city with the occasion flashes within them.

Bubba and I stood in the door with our gear next to us as the train rolled into the Dallas switchyard. A steady rain hammered the top of the boxcar like rapid machinegun fire, and dripped into the doorway, getting our feet wet.

"It's just after four, Bubba said. "The buses won't be running for a couple more hours."

After the train came to a squeaky stop, followed be a loud pssst, we jumped down and started making our way through dreary wet corridors.

Why now, I thought. *We haven't seen a drop of rain, since Eugene.*

"Welcome home," I said jokingly.

"It rains a lot harder than this at times."

"Of course it does. Everything's bigger in Texas, even the rain."

"Yeah and don't forget it," Bubba said, as he stuck out his chest. Then he strutted around like a peacock.

"I'm gonna miss ya kid," I said.

"I'm gonna miss ya too Mike. And I'm gonna miss riding these damn dirty old freight trains. I can't explain it, but riding 'em seemed to have somehow gotten into my blood."

"No need to explain. I understand. But I still better never see you're sorry ass out here running up and down these tracks. If I ever catch you, I swear, I'm gonna give you a woopin' you won't forget, Bubba Lee!"

"I promise I'm gonna to stay put at my dad's until I graduate."

""That's all I wanted to hear. After high school you're on your own kid."

We climbed over dozens of strings of cars, and weaved through the narrow corridors in search of a way out of the steel maze before we found a service road. We came out near a high overpass bridge. Next to the bridge's abutment was a dry place to crash for a couple of hours, so we stretched out on top of our sleeping bags to grab a cat nap.

"Man I'm glad to be off that damn train, Bubba said. "That was the ride from hell."

"Let's just say, I won't be forgetting it anytime soon," I laughed

A switch engine startled me awake as rumbled past. It was also getting light and the sound of traffic was heavy on the bridge above us. I yawned, stretched, then got up and packed. Bubba was still fast asleep.

"Come on kid," I said, nudging him. "You've got a bus to catch. Tonight you'll be as snug as a bug in your own clean warm bed." That grasped his attention. He jumped up and packed up like the madman that he was.

It was still drizzling when we walked out from under the bridge. A ways down from it, we found a path that on the side up the side of a hill that led up into a residential neighborhood. Once out of the neighborhood we didn't have to walk far to find a bus bench. Although the bench was soaked, we sat down anyway.

"I guess this is where we part roads, my friend and blood brother,"

"You're not gonna go home with me, and meet my dad," Bubba said almost in tears. You can come and live us. My dad won't care."

"That's a generous offer, but I know in my heart that my presence wouldn't be appropriate. Neither would it be for me to take you home. I feel you shouldn't even tell your dad how you got back home, at least not for a while."

"How can you say those things   after all we've been through together?"

"More than anything, I wanted to take you to Wishram.   You would have loved it there. There's such a peace about that place. And I wish we could have traveled the nNation together.   I know we would have had a grand old time.   And I wish we could have ridden the high line, the old Great Northern railway that was built by none other than the late great, Mr. James Jerome Hill, the empire Builder himself."

"That's the man Buzz told us about," Bubba said with excitement.

"That'd be the one and only."

"Our journey was the adventure of a life time, wasn't it?"

"Yeah, it was an incredible adventure.   I'll never forget it, or you."

"Nor will I," Bubba said almost in tears. I want you to have my hat to remember me by. And I want you to give my sleeping bag to someone who needs it. Don't think I don't appreciate everything you've done for me, because I do. Being on the road has changed the way I view life altogether. I'll never be the same."

"That's some heavy duty thinking coming from a fifteen year old," I said in awe.

"Don't make fun."

"I'm not. I'm proud of you, kid. I believe the road has taught you humility towards humanity. That's a good thing."

"Yeah, maybe."

"I know you're not the same little cocky, mule headed peckerwood I met back in Yakima. You've come a long way since then."

"Think so?"

"I know so."

A pang of sadness came over me when I looked up and saw the bus coming down the street. A few seconds later it pulled up and came to a squeaky stop. A gush of warm air rolled out when the door flung open. Bubba stood up and stepped toward it. Just as he was about to step inside, he turned around and ran over and threw his arms around me sobbing.

"I'll never forget you!" he sobbed.

Then he turned around, squared his shoulders, wiped the tears from his eyes with his shirt sleeve and proceeded to march on board the bus with the dignity of royalty. As the bus drove away, I watched tear streamed face, pressed against the rear window of the bus until he vanished behind a cloud of diesel smoke. As quickly as he came into my life he was now gone. Something warm ran down the side of my cheeks and it wasn't rain either. I plopped down on the cold wet bench. I had been alone many times throughout my travels, but it had been quite some time since I had felt utterly, and miserably lonely.

"So long my forever friend and blood brother. May God's speed be with you wherever you fare?"

CHAPTER 25

Pulling more than a mile of railcars behind, the five black monster locomotives screamed in agony as they inched at a snails pace, up toward the Continental Divide. For the last couple of hours I'd been intently watching the long freight train twist around and around the sharp switchback curves, on the side of the mountain, like a long steel snake. Now only feet from conquering the eleven thousand foot summit, I stood awed as I gazed out my boxcar door. Cradled between the arms of the mountains far below was a panoramic view of the entire Denver valley. The basin floor and surrounding foothills were adorned with millions of winking shimmering lights. And far out on the eastern plain, I could also see first light beginning to spread out across flatlands like a crimson inferno, while the valley still lay blanketed under a canopy of stars.

In all my travels, I couldn't remember witnessing anything quite so indescribable. *If Curtis were here to see this, he'd be dancing around the boxcar yelping like a lunatic.* The thought brought a smile.

Reminiscing back, I felt compelled to pull out my journal and make a final the entry of our incredible journey.

Two days have come and gone since Curtis and I parted roads, back in Dallas. Yet it seems more like a couple of months. The image of his tear streamed face plastered against the back window of the city bus still haunts me.

After parting roads that dreary morning, I caught a city bus to downtown Dallas. Then I found the nearest Laundromat and spent my last couple of bucks. Later that afternoon, I made my way over to the Burlington Northern switchyard near downtown, only to find out there were no northbound trains due to depart until early the next morning. So I hung out in the Amtrak railroad depot. After dark I ducked into an entryway of an abandoned building across the street from the Burlington Northern, switchyard to take cover from the unmerciful northeastern that kicked up earlier that evening. The building was also as a vantage point to keep an eye on the yards activities. But when I stepped inside, I found a homeless woman curled up in a corner sleeping, clutching a huge suitcase twice her size in one hand. She only had a light coat covering her. Shear terror was in her eyes when she startled awake and saw me standing over her. But I gave her a warm smile to let her know, I wasn't there to harm her. I couldn't help but to feel compassion for her. I assumed everything she owned was either draped over her back, or packed inside her grungy beat up luggage. So I unhooked Curtis's sleeping-bag from my pack and rolled it out next to her, while motioning her to take possession. When she stood up, I realized how petite and frail she really was. Somehow she reminded me of my own sweet mother.

"Go ahead," I said. "Take it, it's yours."

She glared at me with suspicion for a moment. Then she stood up and then burrowed down inside the army issue sack. As she lay there warm and snug, she looked up and beamed the most beautiful warm smile. It was all I could do to keep from choking up. I guarded over her until just before dawn. Then I slinked off into the shadows of the yard to catch my northbound.

From Dallas, I eventually made my way up to Denver, Colorado. In the Denver & Rio Grande western switchyard, on my way to catch a westbound over to Salt Lake City, I bumped into a black man. He was parched from thirst and I was starving. He introduced himself as Isaac. Then he split the only food he had, a bologna sandwich. In return I shared the little water in my possession. We stood in the shadows and talked about our loved ones back home for a while. Isaac was a working family man from Alabama. But on occasion, he was also beckoned by the call of the lonesome whistle and took to the open road periodically. I enjoyed his laughter and his southern style seinsce of humor. As we talked it was plain to see that we were kindred spirits. Isaac and I not shared not only time, more importantly we shared the meal of comaraderiecamaraderieely together.

If we, as people really want to obtain true riches in life, it's important we're kicked out of our comfort zone from time to time. Although my pockets are empty and holes are worn in the soles of my shoes, and I don't have a penny, to my name, I'm a wealthy man. I hold within me many the treasured memories of the people who touched my life all across America. Throughout many travels, I have found something far more valuable than gold or silver and more powerful than all nuclear weapons of mass destruction in this world, I have found love all over America, even from the other side of the tracks. Most importantly I haved discovered that there is a God, who is alive and well.

As I sit here in the boxcar, I can visualize thevisualize the faces of countless people who have touched my life all across America. **life all across America.**

Screeching brakes pulled me from my thoughts. The train had already made the hump and was descending down the western slope.

A frosted meadow glistened under the rising sun like diamonds. And the amber twilight reflected upon the mirrored surface of a nearby pond. As the engines made a crossing, the lonesome whistle echoed out across the void. Once again I remembered why I loved the freedom of the road. I put down the journal and then poked my head out the open door and yelped out a couple of yee-haws in Curtis's remembrance. It had been a long journey and now my faithful bedroll beckoned me like an old friend. I yawned, stretched, and then burrowed deep inside the old familiar down sack. As I lay there, the image of Curtis's tear streamed face pressed against the back window of that Dallas city bus came back to haunt me once again. I'd never forget him or our great adventure we embarked upon together. As long as his blood flowed in my veins, I knew he'd always be with me in spirit and in my dreams. But now it was time to close that segment in the book of my life and begin a fresh chapter, to look forward to the new adventures lurking around the next bend. Then I then rolled over. My final thought before surrendering to the soothing rhythm of the steel wheels beneath, was the world was in my hands traveling so free across her wondrous lands: Clickety Clack! Clickety Clack! Clickety Clack! Clickety Clack!

Ramblin' Railroad Blues

I'm dirty & raggedy goin' westbound,
With the early dawn at my back,
Listenin' to my favorite sound,
Clickety clack! Clickety clack!

I have empty pockets & holes in my shoes,
What the hell, I've nothing loose.
The world is in my hands,
Travelin' so free across her wondrous lands.

When I hear the lonesome whistle blowin',
I've got to pack my bags & roam.
Doesn't matter where I'm goin',
Where ever I lay my hat is my home.

Most say that I'm mad!
Only if they could taste this life so free,
I'm sure they'd be glad,
When their eyes were opened to see.

With new adventures lurking around every bend,
Life is so alive & exciting
I often find it hard to comprehend.
Come on! Doesn't it sound enticing?

I'm dirty & raggedy goin' westbound,

With the early dawn at my back.
Just listenin' to my favorite sound,
While ramblin' down this old railroad track:
Clickety Clack! Clickety Clack! Clickety Clack!

Mike Feistel

GLOSSARY:

Ballast: The gravel used beneath the tracks of railroad beds.

Bindle: A bedroll.

Bridger: A hobo who rode both steam-powered and diesel powered trains.

Bull: Railroad detective

Catch the westbound: To pass away.

Consist: All the cars that make up a particular train

Coupler: Used to connect one train car to another.

Courtesy call: A night's stay in the local jail without being arrested, also an opportunity to get out of the cold and eat a hot meal.

Crummy: The caboose.

Dick: Another term for a railroad detective.

Drag: A slow freight train.

Dumpster diving: Rummaging through dumpsters behind stores, looking for food or other needed items.

Gay cat: A person on the road who, when the going gets tough, can afford to purchase a train, or bus ticket.

Go into the hole: To pull unto a siding to allow another train of higher priority to pass.

Gondola: A train car with low walls and no roof.

Gun boat: An empty can that is used for cooking over the camp fire.

Harness Bull: A railroad detective in uniform.

Helper: One or more engines added to a train to assist in   pulling, or pushing over a steep grade.

High iron: The track in a switchyard that serves as the main or through line.

Hooverville: Shantytowns built of junk and cardboard by the poor, named after Herbert Hoover, the 31st president of the Untied States of America (1929 – 1933).

Hotshot: A fast high priority train.

Jack rollers: Thieves who often target hobos who had just received their pay.

Jocker: A man who travels the road with an underage boy.

Jungle: An encampment where hobos stay for brief periods before moving on. "To jungle up" is to stay in a jungle."

Jungle buzzard: Someone in a hobo jungle who tries to avoid sharing in the work as well as the expense.

Knee shaker: A handout on a plate at the backdoor of a house, eaten on the back steps while balancing the plate on their knees.

Live train: Railcars with the engines already hooked up that could move at moment.

A milk train (local train): A train that makes many stops and does a lot of work in a short distance.

Lump: A handout which is packaged to be taken on the road.

Mission stiff: A bum who spends a great deal of time in the missions.

Mixed freight: Train consisting of a variety of different kinds of freight.

Pearl diver: A dishwasher.

Reefer: A refrigerated freight car.

Rods: The steel structural bars that were below the old boxcars, a very dangerous and difficult place for hobos to ride.

Rule of the match: An insulting gesture of handing a match to someone, as to say, "You are not welcome here at this jungle fire, go build your own someplace else.

Scoping the drag: Looking for a good ride on a freight train when slowing down.

Sit down: A meal given as a handout with the offer to eat in comfort at the table.

Stack train: A train made up of topless, low sided cars which carry large containers sometimes stacked two high.

Independent Authors need readers like you to get the word out about their books. You can support author Mike Feistel by going to www.amazon.com to rate America From The Other Side Of The Tracks. Just type Mike Feistel into the Amazon search bar, choose the paperback edition, and click reviews. Then click create to leave your own review!